# The Angels In Between

## The Book of Muse

# The Angels In Between

## The Book of Muse

Marcia Brennan, Ph.D.

AXIS MUNDI
BOOKS

Winchester, UK
Washington, USA

First published by Axis Mundi Books, 2013
Axis Mundi Books is an imprint of John Hunt Publishing Ltd., Laurel House, Station Approach, Alresford, Hants, SO24 9JH, UK
office1@jhpbooks.net
www.johnhuntpublishing.com
www.axismundi-books.com

For distributor details and how to order please visit the 'Ordering' section on our website.



ISBN: 978 1 78279 114 0



A CIP catalogue record for this book is available from the British Library.

Design: Lee Nash

Printed in the USA by Edwards Brothers Malloy

If you are experiencing a health-related condition, seek appropriate guidance from a qualified professional. The author of this book does not dispense medical advice or prescribe the use of any technique as a form of treatment for physical or medical problems. If you use any of the information in this book, the author and the publisher assume no responsibility.

# CONTENTS

# Also by Marcia Brennan

*Words Beyond Words: Finding Language at the End of Life*. Bristol, UK: Intellect Books, forthcoming.

*The Day Your Heart Broke In Your Eyes*. Nevada City, CA: Blue Dolphin Publishing, 2011.

*Curating Consciousness: Mysticism and the Modern Museum*. Cambridge, MA and London: MIT Press, 2010.

*Flowering Light: Kabbalistic Mysticism and the Art of Elliot R. Wolfson*. Houston: Rice University Press, 2009.

*Modernism's Masculine Subjects: Matisse, the New York School, and Post-Painterly Abstraction*. Cambridge, MA and London: MIT Press, 2004.

*Painting Gender, Constructing Theory: The Alfred Stieglitz Circle and American Formalist Aesthetics*. Cambridge, MA and London: MIT Press, 2001.

*To my husband, Scott Brennan,*
*The Angel who makes everything possible*
*and*
*To my brilliant teacher, Pat McKenna,*
*In joy and gratitude*

*Corda Oculosque Tolle*

Lift Up Your Heart and Your Eyes

# Acknowledgements

With love and gratitude, I would like to thank my husband, Scott Brennan, who has been by my side every step of the way as a source of love and brilliance. I would also like to thank my dear friend and teacher, Pat McKenna, whose presence truly is a gift from the Angels. Without them, this book would never have been written.

For many years, David Carson and Jeff and Julie Kripal have provided valuable support and encouragement, as have my friends Karen Cottingham and Jennifer Wheler, and my sister Camille Gagliardi. Scott McGill contributed his linguistic expertise, and Mitch Horowitz offered excellent editorial advice. I would especially like to thank the team at John Hunt Publishing for their collective expertise in making this book a realization. I am grateful to Maria Moloney, Maria Barry, and Krystina Kellingley for providing valuable suggestions on the text, to Trevor Greenfield and Stuart Davies for their skillful editorial production, to Nick Welch for designing a beautiful book cover, and to John Hunt for his overall support of the project.

Close to home, my beautiful cats Luna and Nicholas were constant companions throughout the writing process. And just as the book would not exist without the support of friends and family, it would also not exist without the love and guidance of the angelic realm. I would particularly like to thank my guide Samson who coordinates interactions at the etheric level, and St. Therese, who wraps the power of the heavens in the sweetness of the flowers. Both last and first, my gratitude goes to the Archangels Ariel, Azrael, Haniel, Matthew, Michael, and Raphael, who are nothing but love in all its glory.

# I

# How to Recognize the Light in Yourself and in Others: Mystical Vision and Knowledge

# 1

# Introduction

## Ideas are Our Familiars: Seeing What We Already Know

Have you ever had the experience of hearing someone say something, or of coming across a seemingly random item that just happens to catch your interest, and thinking to yourself: Oh, yes, I already knew that? It feels like, somehow, you're familiar with a subject even before you've come across it consciously. The ideas can be a helpful reminder of something you need to remember, or they can present intriguing knowledge and even great wisdom on a subject you already knew something about. Just as a part of you immediately picks up on the ideas and embraces them as novel, another, deeper part absorbs this information in a kind of double take because you sense the traces of familiarity. This doubling of knowledge is like looking at an image *and* at its afterimage. It feels like seeing twice, because you're simultaneously sensing novelty and familiarity. Out of your two eyes you are looking at the twin poles of creation and recognition, and the view is quite inspiring.

The two responses follow so closely on the heels of one another that it almost feels as if they are happing simultaneously, but not quite. There is a split second between the two reactions, and in the split of that second, in that crack of consciousness, there is an opening into the metaphorical and the metaphysical realms. This in between space is the composite consciousness of mysticism. Reading *The Angels In Between*—and taking its messages to heart—can help to inspire such consciousness in you. This book is filled with stories drawn from my own experiences, all of which provide vivid examples of how to engage with the metaphorical, metaphysical, and angelic realms. Angels are intermediaries who inhabit the subtle space in between familiar reality and the truth of love, assistance, healing, and grace. In turn, metaphorical language and metaphysical vision grow in and out of the cracks in the familiar surfaces of everyday existence, much like moss grows in the cracks of stones and sidewalks. Cool and green, all it needs is a little shade, and it gives so much hope.

This is why I was inspired to write this book—to give hope and to encourage new growth. Above all, I wanted to tell a story that I couldn't tell elsewhere. I am a tenured Associate Professor of Art History and Religious Studies at Rice University in Houston, Texas, where my scholarship and teaching engage the fields of modern and contemporary art history and museum studies, the medical humanities, and the study of religions and comparative mysticism. I am the author of several books in these areas and the lead author of two museum exhibition catalogues. Since early 2009, I have also served as an Artist In Residence in the Department of Palliative Care and Rehabilitation Medicine at the M. D. Anderson Cancer Center. In that capacity, I work as a creative writer with individuals at the very end of life, and with their caregivers. Through both my scholarly research and my personal and professional experiences, I have come to know the various ways in which a mystic is a person who is able to be in multiple places simultaneously, and who is able to express transformational and transcendent visions. It is my privilege to live and work in many worlds at once. Perhaps this is a familiar story, one that you already know, even as the narrative is expressed in a different form. As you read, perhaps you are seeing some things twice and encountering ideas that are already your familiars.

*The Angels In Between* is like a small psalm of spiritual belief, a little autobiography of divine exposure. This book is about Angels, and it is about my spirituality. In this volume I tell the story of how I, as a professional woman, a trained intellectual, and a professor of the humanities came to my spiritual beliefs through direct personal experiences that inspired an almost overwhelming sense of love, wonder, humility, joy, and gratitude. Each chapter represents an exploration of love, magic, blessings, and a sense of being one with the one face of the universe. As such, this shorthand book of self-dedication tells of the metaphorical and the metaphysical worlds. Everything I write is something that actually happened, and the text is often effervescent.

Through the stories, the Angels offer both practical suggestions and spiritual guidance. At the opening of each chapter, I briefly explain the larger theme and how it can help bring forth the mystic in you. The chapters are followed by practical exercises to further develop and enhance your own skills.

The book addresses six key areas, including:

- How to recognize the light in yourself and in others, so that you can see mysticism as an expanded form of vision and knowledge
- How to cultivate conscious attunement to the angelic world
- How to draw on the mystical and angelic realms to practice the arts of allowance and self-overcoming, which can help to heal old patterns and promote new growth
- How to connect with the mystical dimensions of the natural world and acknowledge the spiritual value of environmental concerns
- How to recognize the mystical dimensions of end of life experience and how to help people leave with grace
- How to live like a Light Carrier

### *Coming Up In Our Feathers*

Have you ever read a book that gave you a powerful sense of

uplift because it showed you that you could walk through your life while being conscious of spirit presence? The Angels say that such books give us a bounce upward from the dense, heavy energies of the world and help us to feel lighter, as if we're coming up in our feathers. We can achieve this lightness of being by letting go of the idea that we are not good enough to do the work of promoting clearing, cleansing, teaching, and healing. In part, this entails going beyond what our conscious personalities thought we could do. The stories in this book are offered as examples to encourage you to be a person who loves, and to open your mind and know that it is possible to change the future through love.

A few years ago, a little after New Year's Day, I had a lucid dream in which I was standing outside gazing at the nighttime sky. As I looked upward, I saw a large star twinkling in the soft black sky. The star sparkled with flashing blue-white and silver light, as very bright stars will do. Then as I watched closely, the star broke apart into tens of thousands of pieces that fell from the heavens. Many of the pieces fell into me and merged with me. I saw that, like so many people here now—like so many of you—I am a Light Carrier, a vessel and a vehicle carrying fragments of starlight inside my being.

This was my New Year's dream of broken starlight, and it relates closely to how I read, how I write, and how I meditate. A separate chapter of this book is devoted to meditation, so at the outset I'll just note that, very often when I am reading, I see bright patches of silver-white, electric blue, and pale lavender light pop and sparkle on the printed page before my eyes. Similar things happen when I'm sitting at my desk writing. I will sometimes see sparkling flashes of colored light on the pages directly in front of me, and I will often see these flashes appear as long columns of light in the corners of my office. These sparkling lights have been with me throughout the writing of *The Angels In Between,* and you may also see lights flashing on the pages as you read, as well. I hope that reading this book can help you to think like a mystic and to live with the Angels, and that as you read, you will be inspired to lift up your heart and your eyes.

# 2

# Seeing Auras: A Day (Un)like Any Other: Seeing Auras at the Post Office

Auras are the visible halo of golden-white light that we all bring with us into the physical world. I'll never forget the first time I consciously recognized that I was seeing auras when I looked at other human beings. It was a powerful spiritual awakening. This experience taught me to see that all human beings—including myself—are composed of both substance and light. While our physical bodies may look quite different on the outside, we all walk with a similar golden-white aura that both permeates our bodies and extends well beyond the individual differences that characterize our appearances. And we carry this light with us wherever we go. With a bit of patience and focus, we can all learn to see auras. The type of viewing described in this chapter can be practiced anywhere where there are bright, neutral surfaces and a natural light source. If you look carefully and allow your gaze to soften, with practice you will be able to see auras around all people, including yourself.

This story happened several years ago. It was an early fall afternoon, and I was standing in a long line at the local Post Office. As usual, I had far too many things to do, including getting a large business envelope out of my hands and into the mail. While several postal workers assisted people at the various stations that ran up and down the long service counter, for some reason, that afternoon the line was really long and it moved very slowly. Between twelve and fifteen people stood in line ahead of me, and they all appeared to be carrying over-sized envelopes like my own—or, even worse—large packages that looked like they would require substantial time and effort to mail.

The more I thought about the situation, the more annoyed I

became, and I contemplated how long I could possibly be stuck standing in line at the Post Office. This train of thought prompted me to reflect on how I was "always so damned busy. This seems to be the story of my life. And all I really want is to get this heavy, bulky thing into the mail so that I can go home and have a nice cup of tea." Then I started considering what type of tea I would have—English Breakfast…Holiday Blend… Chocolate Coconut—and these thoughts made me feel much better until I looked up again and noticed that the line had barely moved. I felt my annoyance turn to anger, and I began to sense little splinters of red hot energy erupt within me. Dammit.

And then I caught myself. I began listening to the internal guidance that was working so hard to get my attention and shift my thoughts in a positive direction. I quickly realized that the best approach would be to cool down and remain patient, so that I could actually use this time wisely to get some of the peace that I needed. As it turned out, there were very good reasons for adopting this internal shift of perspective, as there were other, far more important things I needed to see that afternoon.

So there I stood, waiting in line with the envelope. I took a deep breath, and I felt myself cool down physically and emotionally. My mind began to relax and soften. I'm not sure how long I stood like this, but I do know that, when I looked up again, I saw something extraordinary. The postal worker standing at the counter directly in front of me appeared to be glowing with a subtle pale golden light that resembled a halo. This golden-white light looked like a softly rounded field that extended a few inches around his physical body from the waist up, as that was as much as I could see of him from behind the service counter. While this luminous field was visible all around him, it was brightest and most clearly defined around his head and shoulders. At first I wondered whether this could be a strange reflection or a tricky shadow of some kind, so I kept watching the figure closely. I observed that the light moved as the man moved, and that the movements of the light corresponded precisely with the movements of his physical body as he walked back and forth behind the counter and extended his arms to receive a package. I also noticed that, as he leaned forward to serve a customer, his light reached out to that person, as well. *Oh My God!* I thought to myself, as I stood in total fascination and amazement.

Then I began to wonder whether it was only this particular man who had a golden-white halo around him, or whether other people had them, as well. So, I looked closely at the postal worker in the next station, and I saw exactly the same phenomenon. A luminous field of golden-white light glowed around this diminutive woman, and the light moved as she did. Wherever she went she took her light with her, as it were, as she bent forward to weigh a box and, a moment later, stretched out her hand to receive payment.

I could see auras so clearly because the postal workers stood in front of large plate glass windows that extended across the façade of the building and provided a natural source of illumination. In addition, the postal workers all wore the same light blue uniforms and they stood against a nondescript counter by a solid white wall. These bright, neutral surfaces made viewing conditions optimal, so it was relatively easy for me to observe auras with my physical eyes. And that's exactly what I did. I just stood there watching in fascination, and then I began to wonder whether this luminous appearance was somehow unique to the people who worked at this particular post office. Following this line of thought, I looked closely at the five or six people who now stood in line directly in front of me. Focusing on the person who was two places ahead, I saw that, sure enough, the same phenomenon was clearly visible, as an elderly lady's physical body corresponded with her light body. At first, it was a bit more difficult to discern and track the auras of the people on our side of the counter because the light conditions were uneven, and there were so many visual distractions. Our side of the counter was a far more varied landscape filled with the competing patterns of the carpet, people's clothing, and various envelopes and packages. Yet I was intrigued, and now I was becoming determined to test the limits of how much I could see. After about a minute of concentrated focus it was clear to me that auric light fields were present and visible around everyone in the lobby. You just had to look for them, more or less closely.

That day I consciously realized that I was seeing people's auras. Intuitively, I also knew that I was witnessing a portion of the light of a person's soul, which resembles a golden orb that resides within, yet extends well beyond, the boundaries of the physical body. This auric light is visible to our physical eyes, and we can also see it internally, in our mind's eye. When the two visions converge so that our physical eyes and our spirit eyes become one, the world appears differently before us. Our hearts, eyes, and minds open wider, and we find ourselves standing in an illuminated world—a world that is made of living light.

I'll never forget how I felt that day that was so like, and yet so unlike, any other. This experience produced a feeling of absolute joy. It was as though the light was coming into my eyes so quickly that I almost couldn't see, yet at the same time, I couldn't stop looking, and I felt a powerful softness and tender acceptance of people in their humanity.

Then it was my turn in line. As I handed the large envelope to the postal worker, I couldn't stop smiling, and the person behind the counter couldn't stop smiling, either. The feelings of joy and gratitude were almost overwhelming. Time slowed down and the physical world became intensely clear and sharply focused before my eyes. I knew that I was standing in multiple places at once as I experienced that actual moment of my life, yet while I was also suspended in a timeless field of lucid recognition.

As I went home and contemplated what I had just seen, my sense of elation was only heightened by the realization that we are *all* living light beings. Each and every one of us. As we see the beautiful light of a person's aura, we come to know, very deeply, that there is always more. There is always more to the world, and there is always so much more to each of us, just as there is always more and more light.

### *Practicing Seeing Auras*

Many of the exercises described in this book build on the fundamental skills outlined in this chapter, so it is crucial to practice regularly and not become discouraged.

1. Practice listening to internal guidance. Develop a state of inner quiet. Turn off the computer, the telephone, and all electronic handheld devices. Listen to the silence within and enjoy the inner peace. Begin practicing this skill in a quiet place away from major distractions and external noises.
2. Breathe deeply and slowly, and feel your breath moving inside and outside your body. Enjoy the rhythm of your own breath and the quiet of your mind. Allow your gaze to soften. Do not stare intensely at any one object, but simply allow your eyes to relax.
3. Find a place with a bright natural light source and white or lightly colored walls. Neutral surfaces will cut down on the visual clutter. Begin in a quiet space; later you can practice anywhere.
4. Focus on a person standing five to ten feet away and look closely at their head and shoulders. Allow your soft gaze to focus about an inch above their body, and look for a circular pattern of energy that corresponds with the outline of their physical body, and which moves as they do. An aura is like the luminous counterpart of a shadow. While a shadow is the dark form cast by a solid object, an aura is the bright light that corresponds with a living being.

5. Pay careful attention to how you feel emotionally when you recognize a person's aura.
6. Once you become practiced at identifying auras, notice the variations between people's auras, and the relations between a person's aura and other cues you observe about them. Record your impressions in a journal, and in time you will be able to identify patterns.

# 3

# Recognizing Claircognizance and Clairsentience: The Flash and the Sparkle, and the Light of the Heart

Claircognizance and clairsentience—clear knowing and clear feeling—are mystical qualities that can appear in yourself and in others. Often these characteristics are manifested during early childhood, when we are very sensitive to the seen and the unseen worlds, well before we are told that unseen worlds "don't really exist," or that they only exist in forms and practices that are consistent with established religious traditions. In so many ways, we are taught to forget what we already know intuitively. I hope that reading this story can help you to remember your own deep soul knowledge. This knowledge can help you to hear the many languages that are spoken both on and off the conscious levels.

From the time I was very little, the knowledge of the mind always blended deeply with the knowledge of the heart. I am a clairvoyant, and nearly every day I see spiritual phenomena, yet my primary channels are intellectual (claircognizance) and emotional (clairsentience). Through claircognizance, knowledge and insight come directly into my mind in pristine forms that appear like a flash and a sparkle. Through clairsentience, emotional energies pass directly through my heart center, and often I know empathically what someone is feeling, whether they share their feelings openly or not. I just know things, as I receive the information in my mind and feel the energy in my heart. What this means is that I know and sense what people are really saying behind the words that are spoken aloud. The Angelic Guides have shown me that, beneath the layers of spoken language there lies a second, subtle layer of unspoken language that is composed of thought and energy. So, in addition to seeing things in the split second crack of consciousness that is the double take, I can also read and feel the words behind the words. Yet no matter how much is expressed, I always know that there is so much more than anyone can ever fully know.

It is one thing to write these words as an adult. It is quite another thing to negotiate this territory as a child. One late spring afternoon I sat gazing out the window at the rain that was pouring down on the green grass outside. I was four years old; I wouldn't turn five until later that summer. Our family lived in central Connecticut, and it was very late on a Saturday afternoon. The sky outside was dark gray with thunder and lightning, and I was totally enchanted by the rainstorm. I especially loved seeing the unaccustomed darkness of the daytime sky, and hearing how the wind would speak as it lashed the rain against the windows. The leaves on the maple and oak trees outside were still coming out, and everything was tender, vibrant green and soaking wet. That particular afternoon, during the storm I could actually feel the grass and the bushes growing, and the life energy emanating upward from the ground beneath our feet. I felt such joy and excitement about this new growth, as the gift of the storm brought so much life to life.

My mother was at church, and my little sister was just a toddler napping in her crib, too young to talk with me. I was left at home playing quietly with my dolls, in the care of my Grandmother and a male relative. That afternoon I said to him, "I love days like today. This weather is so romantic." He looked at me strangely, and then he harshly corrected me, saying that the storm was a mess and that there wasn't anything romantic about it. As he said these words, I could feel his annoyance and confusion, bordering on anger, as he told me I was wrong. A part of me was really hurt by this because, apparently, I had gotten it wrong on so many levels at once. I liked something that I shouldn't like because it caused trouble for other people—a violent rainstorm. And I had misused a word and he had to take the time to correct me. Above all, I was wasting his time talking about things that I shouldn't know about, since I was only just a child, and so I was in a state of transgression. (This man had misunderstood my meaning when I said that the storm was "romantic.") In a flash, not only did I hear his words, but I felt his annoyance and hostility, and the energy that his reprimand carried, only some of which was spoken aloud.

Even though I had been told in no uncertain terms that I had gotten it wrong, in my own mind and heart, I also knew that I had gotten it right. While at the time I didn't know what this was, I heard an angelic voice tell me, "Don't you ever, *ever* forget who you are, Dear One." So I knew that it was absolutely right to love this intense spring storm. And I knew that my meaning was right, that the wind and the leaves and the rain *were* romantic in a way that most people did not understand. Yes, I knew I was right, that this storm *was romantic, and that it had something to do with poetry*. Needless to say, as a four-year-old child I had never heard of Romantic poetry. No one had ever introduced the concept to me or read me any of the works of the British Romantic poets. Yet somehow, I just knew. The knowledge was there, both very deeply as well as on the surface of my consciousness. Yet at the same time, I also knew that it wasn't safe for me to say such things aloud. I knew that I needed to protect myself, to remain quiet and not share most things with other people. This was a wise call.

Yet as an enthusiastic child, there were times when I couldn't help myself and things would just come out. Sometimes I was rewarded for this. This happened twice when I was in the first grade. I spent eight years in Catholic school, and one day a young Jesuit priest visited our class to tell us about his mission. It was the early 1970s, and he was planning to lead a walk from Connecticut to Washington, D.C. and hoping to gather supporters along the way to bring attention to Civil Rights issues. After he told the class his story, I raised my hand and asked, "Isn't this like Abraham leading his people to the promised land?" Our first grade class did not have extensive training in Old Testament biblical history (the lessons primarily focused on New Testament Gospel stories), and we had not yet had a lesson on Abraham leading his people. I just knew—I could see the analogy in my mind's eye. Both the nun's and the priest's eyes opened wide and their mouths dropped slightly, and then they started smiling at each other, so I knew I wasn't going to get into trouble. That Sunday morning, another priest told the congregation the story during the sermon at mass. My father was at this church service, and he came home beaming with pride because the priest had mentioned my name when he told the story.

It can pay to know things. Another story which, to this day, is very close to my heart came one Valentine's Day. Our first grade teacher had received some heart-shaped, cardboard candy boxes from the local drugstore for the children to place valentines in. While most of the boxes were a simple plain red cardboard, the store had donated a few boxes that were far more elaborate. They were decorated with either pink or red satin, and they had curly white ribbons and a little cluster of pink or red rosebuds on their tops. Oh, how I wanted one of the decorated boxes, and I was determined to get a pink one! The teacher told us that she would put numbers on the bottoms of those boxes, and if we guessed the number correctly, she would give us that box. As soon as she said those words, the number 14 popped into my mind's eye. I put up my hand and called out the number 14, and she gave me one of the pink heart-shaped boxes. To this day, I can still vividly recall this scene.

So, there were times when having knowledge worked out well. However, most of the time it did not. Neither the other children nor, for that matter, most adults were receptive to anyone who was so different. At a young age I learned quickly not to share things with others, because this could make people uncomfortable and get me into trouble. I grew up in a religious family that was both socially and politically conservative, and as a young girl I had to be very careful talking about things that fell outside of people's comfort zones of knowledge or received social traditions, although sometimes I would do this just to be provocative. Interestingly, I learned that it was okay to talk about magical things on television or in books and movies, because then if everyone could see them, no one felt excluded. Moreover, these subjects could easily be dismissed because everyone knew that they were "only make-believe." Yet deep inside me—in my mind and heart—I knew that aspects of those worlds were very real, just as I knew that I had to keep this knowledge largely to myself. So for my own safety I "turned down the light," as it were, and remained quiet so that I could live "a more normal life."

It took me many years to know that it was safe to see, hear, feel, and know things that were magical and extraordinary, that it was safe to be myself. Yet another part of me still asks: how safe is it really, now or ever? Over the years, I know very well that, because I write so openly about mystical subjects and I am so blatant about my spirituality, that this has cost me something professionally. However, I also know that by living this way, we are all gaining far more than anything I could be losing personally. Interestingly, in the academic world there is still not an adequate way to situate extraordinary knowledge securely, let alone reconcile it with rationalist paradigms. The technical term for such disjunctions of knowledge are "epistemological fractures," and this language is fascinating because it evokes a broken or fractured limb. Indeed, there are days when I have to suppress a lot of what I know and what I'm seeing and feeling, and on those days I have to walk lightly and step very carefully, as though I'm walking tenderly on a healing limb.

Another part of me is hopeful that things are gradually changing. As we consider the relations between rational and intuitive knowledge, we find ourselves poised on the leading edge of what expanded knowledge can mean. I'm hopeful that such multifaceted knowledge can unfold and grow the way that tree leaves do after being lashed by the wind and rain of violent spring storms. Perhaps one day we can all truly know the magic of the rainstorm, and we can be absolutely certain that this knowledge has something to do with poetry.

## *Reading Energy as a Second Language*

### *Remembering*

1. Do you recall childhood experiences when you saw presences that were invisible to others and which may have been dismissed as "imaginary"?
2. Were there times in your childhood when you were dismissed or ridiculed for knowing something that others didn't, but that you knew, sensed, or saw? If so, recall if you sometimes used this information to your advantage.
3. Did you grow up in a particularly religious or skeptical household, where you had to suppress certain knowledge or where you were taught to avoid the unseen worlds?

### *Practicing*

1. In situations where something is about to happen, pause and take a deep breath. Can you guess what it is? How often are your guesses correct?
2. Practice reading the energy behind the words that people speak aloud. As someone says something, understand and sense that they are speaking a second, subtle language of energy that may or may not correspond to the words they are saying aloud.
3. Practice feeling the intuitive difference between a truth

and a lie. For example, using your own name, say aloud, "My name is [state your name]." See how this feels to you. Then repeat this sentence with a name that is not your own. Notice the differentials. Repeat this exercise, paying careful attention to the subtle energy behind the language.

# 4

# Experiencing the Dark Night and the Mystical Reawakening: The Mountains, the Eagle, and the Golden Light

In my book *The Day Your Heart Broke In Your Eyes*, I tell the story of how I experienced a powerful mystical reawakening after receiving my Ph.D. At the time, I had undergone intense personal and spiritual challenges that pushed me beyond the limits of all that I knew. Because this experience is so relevant to the story of how I came to my spiritual beliefs, I will include it here. While this was certainly not easy, one of the very powerful lessons that I learned is not to resist what is difficult because the experience truly can be transformational. Perhaps you, too, have undergone a Dark Night of the Soul, and you will recognize elements of your story in my own.

Shortly after I completed my doctorate at Brown University, I was working hard on turning my dissertation into a first book, while also teaching part-time at the College of the Holy Cross in Worcester, Massachusetts. I was on the job market, looking for my first full-time, tenure track position. In short, I was living in a transitional space—a space between spaces—in my own autobiography.

In many ways, this was a wonderful time, as I had completed one life goal and was working on the next. Yet in many ways, this was also an extremely difficult time. I had entered a hyper-competitive professional arena during the beginning of what would increasingly become a shrinking job market. Moreover, because I work in a popular field, modernist art history, there were literally hundreds of distinguished applicants competing for the handful of open positions that arose nationally each year. The more elite the institution, and the more desirable the geographic location, the longer the odds that anyone would successfully win the position, no matter how superbly qualified they might be. (I'll also note that today, with the wide-scale economic cutbacks and the continuing erosion of support for scholarship in the humanities, the employment landscape in academe is even more challenging than the picture I'm painting historically.) To complicate matters further, in the years immediately after I completed my doctorate, a lot of very good jobs were popping up in very remote locations, places where my husband would not be able to sustain a high-tech career, and thus, where he would not be able to join me. Although many professional couples have successful commuter marriages, in my mind it was never an option for us to be separated, even temporarily. In short, these were complicated life decisions, in part because they constantly placed my home and my heart in conflict with my professional and intellectual life.

Yet in my heart, I always knew that this was the right decision, and it was. However, I also knew that this life choice would require greater amounts of patience, endurance, persistence, and faith than I possessed at the time. After a few years had passed and nothing was finalized, hope became increasingly difficult to sustain, and the shadows of doubt grew longer until I could not see my path forward in the darkness of the uncertainty.

Looking back, I now realize that I was walking the path of a Dark Night, as one part of my life, which I loved and cherished, seemed to be closing down around me. Although I could not see it at the time, another part of my life and being were opening, and this opening may well not have happened if my professional life had gone on smoothly, and I did not have to turn inward and look squarely into the eyes of the unknown, knowing full well that I was trying to see a future that I could not see. In the depths of this darkness was the spark of an awakening.

Throughout college and graduate school, my formal

education both emphasized and prized rigorous intellectual inquiry of a sort that left very little room for issues of metaphysics and spirituality. Within the venerable structures of academia, there is often little breathing room for subjects and questions that lie well outside the box, or outside the picture frame, of analytical logic, empirical and historical evidence, and well-established interpretive methodologies. This is especially the case for younger scholars who are working hard to prove themselves within the "safety" of established conceptual structures, while trying to get their careers off the ground.

With some unexpected time on my hands, I began to read more widely than I could have otherwise. As I read, I began to see the wisdom in texts that could not be integrated into the structures of my intellectual training, books that would have been dismissed as essentialist and metaphysical. As the boundaries fell away and the walls came down inside of me, space was created for an expanded sense of vision. While still struggling and moving with difficulty, at least I was moving forward.

This is the backdrop against which the explosion occurred.

It happened one afternoon during the late spring, after the year's job recruiting season had ended. Once again, I found myself struggling emotionally with the prospect of facing another year as a "homeless academic." To take my mind off the situation, my husband and I took a brief vacation to Arizona. We were in Mesa, standing at the base of the Superstition Mountain, a Native American sacred site, and an extraordinary place of beginnings and ends and beginnings again. The mountain road twisted upward, with spectacular views leading to a place called Tortilla Flat. As we drove higher and higher up the mountain, my husband pulled the car over to the side of the road, and he got out to take some pictures of the breathtaking Sonoran Desert scenery. I also got out of the car and walked down the road just a bit, in the opposite direction, to see the mountain from a different angle. And then it happened. As I was gazing outward and upward at the mountains and into the sunlight, a golden eagle flew up very fast behind me, passing directly over my shoulders and landing on a tree branch a few feet away. At first, I was quite surprised and a bit frightened, as golden eagles are not small birds, and this one was very, very close. Yet oddly enough, another part of me was completely at peace and I stood very calm and still. For several minutes the eagle perched directly on the branch in front of me and looked into my eyes. At the time, I knew nothing about the habits of the eagles of Arizona, and so I had no idea how usual or unusual this perching behavior might be. Yet another part of me knew with certainty that something miraculous was happening. All I could do was gaze back in wonder at this magnificent bird, and give thanks for the gift of this unforgettable encounter.

After a while, my husband had his pictures, and we got into the car and began driving down the mountain. That's when it happened, when my view of the world literally dissolved into a vision of fluid light. As we were driving down the mountain, I saw very clearly that the entire mountain landscape was not merely composed of solid rock, but that the mountains were made of light, and that everything was alive. Everything was solid and everything dissolved, and the light became a living presence. There are no words for this, even as I'm trying to find words to translate sacred experience into clear, descriptive language. At the time, I tried to tell my husband what I was seeing, and I could not fully do so; I could only express hints and glimpses. I began to cry softly as I was filled with an overwhelming sense of joy and love and gratitude. That was the day my heart broke in my eyes.

Over time, I came to learn the name of the golden eagle who perched before me in Arizona, and the reason for our encounter. Her name is Mountain Feather, and she came to me as a totem. She called me Daughter, and I was told that Eagle holds the vision, and that from that point onward I would be flying to places where other people could not follow. At the time, it felt like it had taken me forever to reach this place, and now, looking back on that day, it feels like it happened only yesterday. All I can do is express my gratitude for an experience that still brings tears to my eyes. On the day that the mountains melted and turned to light, the Golden Eagle carried a message that I now carry to you:

*"Feel the Freedom Found in Oneness and Let Your Spirit Soar."*

### *Recognizing Transformative Mystical Experiences*

1. Recall a crisis situation in which your sense of identity was called into question, along with the boundaries of what you thought was possible. During these times, did you receive unexpected guidance or inspiration? If so, what form did it take? How were you a different person afterward?
2. Have you ever had unexpected or unusual encounters with a wild animal? If so, what animal was it, and what were the circumstances? How did you feel afterward? Did your life change, even in a subtle way?
3. Have you ever been in situations that were so overwhelmingly beautiful that you felt at a loss for words? How do you find words to describe these experiences today?

# 5

# Seeing Dreams as Vehicles of Communication and Divine Guidance: The Islands in the Sky and the Jewels Beneath Our Feet

There are many different types of dreams, including lucid dreams that can represent sources of inspiration, creative insight, and divine guidance. Dreams can serve as important vehicles of communication, and sometimes they forecast the future. Dreams can also show us the complex ways in which a visionary world resonates with actual, lived existence.

Several years ago, while I was still opening my mind to the possibility of the psychic world, I had a very powerful precognitive dream. This lucid imagery arose in the fragile boundary between sleeping and waking—which is itself a crack in time and an opening between states of consciousness. Everything appeared in a vibrant state of hyper-clarity.

I dreamed that I was me, living my normal life. I looked exactly like myself, and I was standing in front of the Rockefeller Library at Brown University. It was an ordinary day and I was doing familiar things, including teaching classes and doing research at the library. As I stood in front of the Rockefeller Library talking with some friends, I looked up and I saw an amazing sight. Hovering in the sky above us was a group of incredibly beautiful islands. Each was a miniature world, a little landscape filled with intricate formations of boulders and rocks, lush green trees and delicate ferns. Nestled between the rocks and the plants were flowing waterfalls, and the intricate rock formations resembled sculptures. Each hovering island was its own sustainable world with its own miniature ecosystem. While this description is insufficient, in the dream the islands in the sky reminded me a bit of very elaborate bonsai gardens, miniature worlds that are cultivated as self-contained, contemplative microcosms. Yet in the dream, the islands in the sky were infinitely larger and more elaborate than any bonsai garden. Each was a world unto itself, even as together, they formed a community. As I studied the islands in the sky more closely, I noticed that the bright blue sky simultaneously functioned as air and water; that is, it was the air that my friends and I breathed, just as it was the vast ocean in which the islands gently floated.

In the dream, I was standing on the sidewalk talking with a group of people. When I saw this vision I stretched out my arm and pointed up at the sky and I said to everyone, "Oh My God, look at that! They're so beautiful!" Yet no one else could see what I was seeing. I am a persistent person so, true to myself, I tried again. I pointed upwards even more emphatically and attempted to call people's attention to this incredibly beautiful and unusual sight. Yet to my surprise, frustration, and sadness, not a single person could see the intricate worlds that floated above us, the islands in the sky.

When I awoke from the dream, I knew very deeply that the dream foretold what I would shortly experience. I knew that I would be able to see incredible things that other people could not. I knew that these magical and metaphorical visions would float and hover above us, and that they would be of great intricacy and beauty. Again and again, I would have to discern when it would be wise to remain silent, and when it would be appropriate to tell others what I was seeing and try to share these extraordinary visions.

The dream of the islands in the sky is a vivid symbol of how my mind was changed and my life was changed because I knew that there had to be more than the reality that we all commonly saw with our eyes and reaffirmed as a culture. Over the years, I have questioned myself again and again as I have opened my mind wider and allowed myself to see the mystical and angelic worlds that unfold alongside our human one. These are *not* separate realities, but different facets and dimensions of an expansive continuum of being. All of these openings have made me a better person.

As you can imagine, it is a great privilege to be walking this path, and I wouldn't have it any other way. Yet to be completely honest, it is often very difficult. In my heart I always know that giving up is never an option. That piece of insight became clear when I awoke from the lucid dream of the islands in the sky.

I suspect that, from time to time, many of you reading this book have also found yourself walking this path. I hope very much that these words resonate for you, and that my telling this story provides a sense of clarity and kindredness. We all stand in solidarity with the light as we contemplate the islands in the sky. This is the path forward, just as it's the path upward and beyond.

And just as mystical insights can appear from above, so too can they appear from below—from the ground beneath our feet and in the depths of our consciousness. Indeed, both practical living and inspired dreaming engage the resonance between the worlds above and below, as well as the various thresholds that connect them. Let me give you another example of this lucid metaphorical imagery. In my first job after college, I worked as a Research Assistant, and then as a Research Analyst, at the Massachusetts Institute of Technology (MIT). The university's exterior architecture on Massachusetts Avenue in Cambridge is a formal stone structure with high platforms of stairs leading in to the main entrance. Once you step inside the front doors, you are standing at the edge of "the infinite corridor," a long central hallway that runs the length of the original main buildings. While most people look upward and all around them in this extraordinary environment, it is also worthwhile to look down at the ground. The floor is remarkable, as its smooth, gleaming surface is covered with a mixture of crushed stones. While most of the stones are a light-grayish and white color, embedded in this mixture are also colorful traces of dark olive green and deep burgundy, as well as pebbles of gold and veins of silver. While all of this sounds very ornate, it is actually quite subtle and you have to look closely in order to see it. It is a striking experience to walk the length of the infinite corridor, and when the sunlight strikes the tall windows and gleaming floors at just the right angle, the effects can be dazzling.

On the night when the first words and images appeared for this book, I had a lucid vision. I was shown an image of myself walking down the long hallway of the infinite corridor, and thus, walking on a ground that exists in reality, one that I have literally walked thousands of times, and I recognized the space instantly. Yet in a flash the scene shifted, and I was shown that I was also walking on metaphorical ground. The floor beneath my feet looked ethereal, like a marble cloud with many sparkling gems embedded in its surface. It may have been a vision of the firmament. Once again, you had to look closely in order to discern the gleaming olive green and deep burgundy stones, with silver and gold threads scattered throughout the entire field. Yet I was clearly shown that these gems lie under our feet. Unless you look closely and notice them, you might miss them all together. While they are subtle, they are extremely intense and beautiful.

The Angelic Guides tell me that these scattered jewels represent fragments of our lived experiences, our memories, inspirations, and intuitions of the wisdom embedded deep within us. These sparkling bits of ancient light—of knowledge, creation, and recognition—reside on the metaphorical ground of our consciousness as we walk through our lives. In our lived realities, we walk on many grounds at once as we constantly walk between worlds. The jewels beneath us are radiantly familiar, even though we may not have seen them in quite this way before.

This lucid image is another example of seeing twice, of the double take that shows the power of metaphorical language to convey metaphysical insights. The long stone hallways and highly polished surfaces of "infinite corridors" filled with jewels sparkling in the ground beneath our feet are all vivid metaphors that can help us to recognize the gems of what we already know. Like cherished, magical companions, these ideas are our familiars.

### *Recognizing How Dreams Can Serve as Links between Worlds*

1. Keep a dream journal and record any unusual or vivid dreams as soon, and in as much detail, as possible. Note how the dream makes you feel when you awake. Review the journal periodically to see which dreams were prescient.
2. Notice the state between sleeping and waking. How do you move between these modes of consciousness?
3. Pay careful attention to how objects function as symbols in your dreams. Note whether objects appear from above or below. How does one thing function in many ways at once? Understanding this sense of multiplicity and connection can build your observational skills and serve as a practical link between metaphorical imagery and metaphysical vision.
4. Listen carefully to the stories other people tell of their dreams, and be discerning about whom you choose to share your dreams with.

# 6

# Meditating with the Muse: How to Meditate

At this point in my life, I find it absolutely necessary to have some silence every day, a period of contemplation when I am immersed in complete quiet. During these moments of peace, I allow my vision to open wider to the etheric world, and in these states I have seen and heard some amazing things. In this chapter I describe my own meditation process, which may be helpful in getting you started and providing suggestions for how to access the higher visions that can emerge in contemplative states. At the outset, I'll emphasize that this is just my own practice, and there is no one right way to do this. Indeed, there are an infinite number of pathways.

Many years ago I learned that meditation is a corridor of consciousness that can provide a gentle and effective way to connect human beings with the heaven world. At that time, I was reading metaphysical literature fairly broadly, and I was spending time in Arizona, where I was drawn to many Native American subjects. Yet it was not until I returned to Boston and I was browsing in a local bookstore that I came across Mary Dean Atwood's book *Spirit Healing: Native American Magic & Medicine*. While the text offers many useful discussions of spiritual subjects, it was actually just a few pages of this book—really, just one section of one chapter—that changed my life. In these few pages, the author gave clear and practical steps for a meditation practice. Today I don't follow any predetermined method, nor do I stick to the specific interpretations that this author offers of colors, animal symbols, etc. What matters is that Dean's accessible book got me started in a very effective way.

When I meditate I like to allot at least half an hour to this practice, and I like to meditate in the morning before I begin my other work for the day. I meditate in my office, where I have a clear, level wooden desk facing windows that open onto the back garden. Before meditating, I open the shades so that I have natural sunlight coming into the room, and it is very quiet—I have turned off the ringer on the telephone because one thing that does not work well for me is to be jarred abruptly between states of consciousness. In short, in the mornings my office is a shaded yet sunny oasis of quiet, calm, and peace. I sit quietly at my desk, and typically I have a sheet of paper and a pen available at my right hand. Oftentimes, I have found that important guidance comes when I am in meditation, and it is necessary for me to make brief, sketchy notes and record specific phrasings of words so that later I can remember what I am shown and transport this intelligence between worlds.

Sometimes it can be helpful to work with a physical prop, which can serve as a touchstone to ground and center your thoughts. On my desk I have a very beautiful amethyst whose surface is covered with crystals, and I place this open geode directly in front of me. During the meditation, I place both hands lightly on either side of the stone; it's almost as if my fingers are the prongs of a setting that holds the jewel. While this stone is not absolutely necessary for my meditation, I have found that its familiar presence helps me to enter a mode of peace and uplift more quickly because it provides a supportive reference point in the physical world as I connect with the spirit world.

Then I close my eyes, take some deep breaths, and the meditation begins. I always begin by thanking the Angelic Guides with my whole heart for all that they do, for all that they are, for all that is and for all that will be. Both the beginning and the ending of the meditation are expressions of love and gratitude. Then, I tell the Angelic Guides very clearly about the situation that I am requesting help or guidance with. Of course, they already know the situation more fully than I do myself. Yet my stating the situation to them actually represents my stating the situation to myself, to clarify it in my own mind while consciously recognizing that I am asking for assistance. As I sit quietly and breathe, giving thanks for angelic insight, I find that I become very clear and peaceful.

What happens next is amazing: I watch as the light starts to shift behind my eyes. In meditation I will go from seeing nothing—that is, simply seeing the darkness of my own closed eyelids—to seeing a field of gently swirling blue-violet and purple light. The light moves of its own accord, and it often has gold around the outer edges, appearing as if it is haloed. I have found that if I pay attention to the light rather than to the angelic conversation, I will lose the connection, so I need to stay focused on what brought me into the meditation in the first place. This shifting field of violet light is a contemplative space of great wisdom and insight. When I'm sitting in this space, it's as though I'm able to fly above a situation and see it with a bird's eye view, rather than only walking as an actor on the earth below. When I'm flying above a situation, I'm able to see life from an elevated perspective, and in that state I can see another person's point of view. Often, it will appear as though I'm looking out through their eyes, knowing what's in their mind, and feeling what's in their heart. Even though I can see and feel things, there is a sense of detachment regarding what is occurring. It's almost as if I'm not in a framework of personal human consciousness, but in an elevated state of spiritual neutrality. Sometimes what I'm shown is not pretty, but it does give me tremendous insight and understanding into what is happening and why this is so. Very often there is a sense of revelation and I tell the Guides, "Wow, that never would have occurred to me, but it makes total sense now. Thank you." With this understanding often comes a shift of perspective, which is followed by compassion. Again, it's very helpful to have pen and paper at hand, so that I can make notes to remember what I am shown after I leave this meditative state.

With practice, I have learned how to shift between states of consciousness flexibly enough to return to my body to make these quick notes and then glide back up into the contemplative state without losing momentum. This takes a lot of practice, but it is a practical skill that can be mastered like any other.

Sometimes, in addition to asking for guidance, I will ask for insight with my scholarly or creative work. Again, ideas come through that are amazing. Very often, in addition to the shimmering field of blue-violet light, I will see flying sparks of extremely bright silver-white light. The sparkles resemble the little bits of water that fall from the edges of a fountain. I have asked about these falling sparks, and the Angelic Guides have told me that they are "flashes of purity and insight." When I see these falling lights amidst the violet field, I am always filled with a deep sense of love and gratitude.

In the course of writing *The Angels In Between*, I was guided to do a meditation specifically to be included in the chapter on meditation. Here is the message that I was given for you:

Behind my closed eyes, I was told that I was "sitting in my center," and then the Angel of Meditation appeared. He is very tall and clear and extremely beautiful. When entering the contemplative space of meditation, it felt like stepping inside of this Angel himself, as though he invites us into himself. Entering this Angel's presence is like stepping inside a faceted prism or many-sided crystal. He says that, "As you enter a state of meditation, you enter a state of the soul. I help you to become quiet and hold this space of vision." The Angel of Meditation gave me the metaphor of a library or a wonderful bookstore. He told me to see how books can be examples of meditations, because the words reflect an author's perspective. Thoughts come off the pages like lights shining from the various facets of a crystal. The Angel of Meditation wants readers to know that you can call upon him any time to assist in your own meditative states.

This Angel also tells me that meditation is an example of entering the spaces within spaces, because this act allows you to enter a zone of heightened thought and understanding. He asks you to consider that, when you start meditating, please pay attention to how you live in your physical body, and see if you inhabit your body a little differently. See if you carry this heightened energy out of meditation and into your lifestyle, including how you occupy the real estate of your body. Your facial expressions may change slightly. Your heart center may open, and there may be a new softness in your eyes and in your bearing. The Angel of Meditation encourages you to "Take small steps at first, if needed, and see what you see. Know that, as you meditate, you sit inside a sacred dwelling, and the view within is filled with an infinite number of windows that look out on many different realities."

## *Practicing Meditation*

1. Sit in a quiet place. Turn off all electronic devices including your telephone. If other people are around you, tell them that you do not want to be disturbed. Allow at least half an hour for your meditation.
2. Keep a pen and paper by your side to make notes and record ideas.
3. Before entering meditation, determine one question or subject that you would like to examine. Enter your meditation with this clearly in mind.
4. If you have a particular item that serves as a touchstone for you—such as a mineral, a small sculpture, or a book—place this item on the desk in front of you.
5. Close your eyes, breathe deeply, and give thanks for the meditation and all the communications that arise. Then state your question or focus on your issue. Listen carefully. Sitting quietly, see what guidance comes forth.

Be open to whatever appears, especially if it represents an unfamiliar perspective.

6. Pay special attention to any lights, colors, or images that appear behind your closed eyes.
7. You may wish to imagine that you are stepping inside the Angel of Meditation, who is at once a presence, a space, and a state of mind. Know that you can call on this Angel for assistance and guidance.
8. Pay attention to how you live inside your physical body, both while you are meditating and after the meditation is complete.
9. Express gratitude for all of the information and insight that you receive.
10. Know that there is no one right way to mediate, and that you may need to explore a bit to find a meditation practice that works well for you.

# II

# How to Connect with the Angelic World

# 7

# Knowing that You are Always Accompanied: Angels of Accompaniment

How would you live your life differently if you knew that you were not alone, and that help is always available, like a gentle yet radiant light that accompanies you everywhere you go? Such assistance is always available, but you must ask to receive it. Like all of the events described in *The Angels In Between*, this is a true story. Taking this story to heart will help you open up to seeing and feeling the Angels who accompany you throughout your life. This story can also help you sense how to act in partnership with the angelic world, and how to accompany others if you are guided to do so.

Early one afternoon, I was traveling on the Metro Rail train on my way in to work at the hospital. The sky was an ominous dark gray with a wall of thunderclouds hovering in the east. My primary concern was that it didn't rain violently and flood the tracks before my train could reach its station, which is situated at a particularly low-lying point in the medical center. As the train traveled through the various stops along the route of the Texas Medical Center, I noticed a middle-aged Asian woman tentatively rise from her seat and approach the door, all the while gazing anxiously around her. In addition to her uncertainty about which stop she was looking for, this slight woman seemed a bit unsteady on her feet, as the jerky motions of the train made her struggle slightly to maintain her balance. I sat nearby, wondering if there were a gentle and tactful way that I could offer to help this woman. And then I saw an Angel appear beside her. The Angel stood directly behind the woman, and the tips of its beautiful, long tapered fingers appeared like a flashlight that directed the woman's gaze to the map above the door showing the various stops along the train route. The Angel placed a white light around one of the stations, indicating the correct Metro stop for her. This Angel also helped to steady the woman's gait and support her stance more solidly.

The woman was being assisted by an Angel of Accompaniment. Angels of Accompaniment are guiding angels. This particular Angel looked like a candle, with an extremely tall, slender white body that he used to support and steady the woman, and long white fingers with luminous tips. The Angel's golden head glowed like the sun, shedding light so that the woman would see the map of the Metro route and recognize the correct stop. A bright halo of light surrounded this woman because this Angel of Accompaniment provided such wonderful guidance and support. Part of his assistance included drawing my attention to the woman so that I could offer to help her, as well. Very gently, with words that I received in my mind and felt in my heart, the Angel asked me if I would assist this woman as she got off the Metro and escort her to the correct hospital building. I was more than happy to do so. It made me so joyful, not only that I could provide practical assistance to this woman, but that the human and angelic worlds could collaborate so seamlessly.

## *Experiencing Angelic Accompaniment*

1. During past times of difficulty or uncertainty, can you recall feeling that you were not alone, but that you were accompanied by an Angel? Know that you are always guided and accompanied, and that angelic assistance is always available if you request it. When you are in an unfamiliar location, or if you are feeling uncertain regarding what to expect, call on the Angels of Accompaniment to guide you safely and remain by your side. After requesting assistance, see if you feel differ-

ently, or if you can discern an angelic presence.

2. Much like seeing auras around people, look for bright lights accompanying yourself or others. Angels often resemble moving energy patterns of sparkling white light. While auras correspond to the physical bodies of people and animals, Angels are etheric and thus are typically without a physical component.
3. Does it ever seem like, when you are facing multiple choices, one choice in particular stands out and appears to glow, as if it were surrounded by a bright light?
4. Were there times in the past when someone unexpectedly assisted or accompanied you? How did that make you feel? Have you ever been drawn to guiding or helping someone you didn't know? Or have you been reluctant to do this, or hesitant to receive the help that others have offered you?
5. Pay attention to people around you who may need your help. If you can see them, notice how angelic presences interact with the people they assist.
6. As always, give thanks for all the assistance that you receive.

8

# Seeing Angels: More Beautiful than You can Imagine

In so many ways, the material world that we all inhabit includes a strong symbolic dimension. In turn, the metaphorical aspects of life can be closely related to the metaphysical world, but we have to allow ourselves to see this. Mysticism is an awareness of such composite consciousness, of the many within the one. The stories contained in *The Angels In Between* can help you to cultivate such mystical consciousness. In particular, this chapter can help you to recognize the many forms that Angels can take. Sometimes Angels appear as amorphous light, but other times they assume symbolic forms that are as significant as they are beautiful.

I am often allowed to see angelic presences with my physical eyes, and I always feel so grateful and joyful when this happens. Out of consideration for the normal flow of my life, and the many worlds that I move in professionally, the Angels don't always give me a visible appearance because "we don't want to upset your applecart." They know that I am extremely sensitive, and when we work together they always treat me with such gentleness and care. Yet it is always a gift when I am allowed to see them, either with my outer physical eyes or with my inner spirit eyes, and to know their closeness in my mind and feel their presences in my heart.

I see Angels everywhere, and they take many different forms and appearances. Often their sizes and shapes are determined by what will be most appropriate and effective in a given situation. Sometimes I see the detailed shapes and forms of Angels, and I see them carrying striking symbolic props. Very often I see angelic presences as extremely bright, colorful electric lights that move in a flash. I have seen Angels in every color of the prismatic spectrum, and I have seen colors that are quite unlike the colors that we typically see in this world. The best comparison I can give is that of the iridescent flash of a rainbow moonstone or an opal when their translucent, milky surfaces catch the sunlight at just the right angle, and they give off brilliant flashes of colored light.

### *Extremely Close to Home*

One night I was having trouble sleeping. As I lay in bed in the darkness I turned over on my side. I looked up at the ceiling and, out of the corner of my eye, I saw a configuration of extremely bright amber, gold, and copper-colored lights whirling above me. The angelic light form was very large and constantly shifting. The radiant amber and copper-colored swirls appeared to be flowing as if in a kind of dance. Immediately, I felt warmed and comforted, because I knew that I was accompanied even in my sleep, and that I was being guarded and held in this magnificent swirl of burnished colored light.

Another evening, my husband and I were watching a British murder mystery show in the den. About two-thirds of the way into the program, I looked over and I saw an extremely bright white Angel sitting on the arm of the sofa. The Angel appeared to be watching the program with us. Then I looked back at the television, and I saw another very bright white Angel hovering beneath the ceiling, just to the left of the screen. While these details may seem quite commonplace, they illustrate the wonderful ways in which Angels are woven into the very fabric of our domestic life, as constant and beautiful companions that light our home.

### *Glowing Books and Lighted Candles: Angels and Ceremonial Occasions*

Very often, I see Angels as sparkling orbs of colored light that hover and shimmer in the air. I once asked the Angels why they frequently took on this appearance, and they responded that this is the easiest form for them because it is pure energy. Angels tend to move very quickly, sometimes leaving a trail of sparks that disappear in a flash. At other times, during ceremonies and special events, I have seen powerful Angels standing in a single place for quite a long time. During these special circumstances, the Angels will often assume a form that resonates with the occasion. Once at a friend's wedding, I observed a very large, bright white Angel standing at the right-hand side of the altar beside a cluster of lighted white candles. As beautiful as the bride herself, yet far more etheric, this Angel of Presence was blessing the wedding ceremony, and I knew that she would continue to bless my friend's marriage, as well.

Another time, I was co-hosting a symposium at the university, an event that brought several extremely distinguished scholars to campus to speak on a wide variety of spiritual and artistic subjects. As the afternoon session began, I introduced the first speaker and then I sat down in the front row of the auditorium so that I could listen closely to the lecture. As I settled into my chair, I looked up and, on either side of the stage were two enormous Angels. Their bodies were like luminous anchors, as one stood near the podium by the door, while the other was positioned at the far end of the room at the edge of the long wooden conference table. The Angels were grand and monumental. At first, their shapes were amorphous, and they simply appeared as extremely large fields of glowing light. Then their appearances shifted and they resembled two very large, solid bookends that supported a long stack of colorful, upright books with golden letters on the bindings. Then their appearances shifted again and the Angels looked like two extremely large golden candlesticks standing at either end of a mantelpiece while a fire burned brightly in the grate below.

These transitions all unfolded in the blink of an eye. Yet whatever shape they took, the Angels' forms were transient and etheric, and they remained present throughout the talk. When I looked up again at the end of the presentation, the Angels appeared as they did when I first saw them, as two extremely large and nearly formless fields of glowing light. I am so thrilled and honored that these Angels were present at our gathering, and that our worlds touched one another in this way.

### *The Pink Roses*

Just as human beings are surrounded by Angels, so too are the plants and animals that inhabit the natural world. While a later section of this book is devoted to mystical encounters with nature, I will include a brief example here, in this introductory discussion of Angels.

One semester, I had to teach in a classroom that was located at the far edge of campus. After class ended, my walk home took me through a back service road that ran past several engineering buildings, as well as the physical plant that houses the electrical generating station that powers the campus. Much of this heavy industrial equipment is housed in a large brick building with a tall tower. Yet directly in front of this building is a small, circular garden bordered with bricks, which holds a group of pink rosebushes. I have always been struck by the contrast between this delicate miniature rose garden and the heavy industrial building sitting directly behind it.

One day, as I was walking past the rosebushes, I noticed that one of the plants was in full flower, with gorgeous open clusters of pink blossoms. This sight was so lovely, and it made me feel so happy. While I stared at the roses, I saw with my physical eyes that etheric arcs of pink and golden light were flickering around the sides of the flowers. The rose-pink lights were extremely delicate and beautiful. They resembled tiny, vividly colored sparks that appeared to be dancing around the blossoms. As with all plants, I knew that the beauty of the rosebush was both physical and metaphysical, as I saw both the material form of the flowers and the etheric forms of the fairies, or light beings, who acted as Guardian Angels for the plant.

Such visions always inspire in me a sense of absolute joy and wonder. In this case, these feelings were only heightened because of the striking contrasts. This scene showed me that, even while walking past an industrial building housing heavy machinery, it is possible to see the shimmering divinity of the natural world.

### *Seeing Angels*

1. Just as there are many different types of people, so too are there many different types of Angels. While certain Angels accompany you always, other Angels will appear on special occasions, such as weddings, holidays, ceremonies, or other special events. The next time you attend a wedding, look closely and see if you can discern bright lights or shifting energetic presences around the wedding couple or standing at either side of the altar. Allow your gaze to soften, breathe deeply, and see if you can discern angelic forms. Similarly, the next time you are attending a lecture, watch the area directly behind the speaker, or at either end of the stage, and see if you notice patterns of luminous shifting energy. If you do discern angelic presences, make special note of the forms, context, and location of their appearance, as well as any distinctive symbols or props the Angels are carrying.
2. Angels often make extensive use of symbols. Practice understanding the many meanings of symbols. Reflect on the ways in which a single object can express multiple meanings simultaneously.
3. If you are having difficulty sleeping, ask that an Angel be sent to calm and soothe you. Close your eyes, breathe deeply, and request that an Angel be present. Then see if you feel differently, or if you sense any luminous energies

or presences in the room.

4. You can request that your house be filled with Angels, so that only light can enter your home. Over time, see if you detect any subtle shifts of energy in the house, including a more positive atmosphere.
5. When you are outdoors, look gently at the sides of flowers from a distance of five to ten feet. See if you can discern colorful flickering lights or sparks of energy surrounding blooming plants.
6. As always, pay careful attention to how these events make you feel, and express gratitude for the gift of angelic presences. Keep a careful record of all your experiences.

# 9

# Receiving Angelic Guidance and Indication: The Golden One

As you open your mind wider and wider, so too do you open your heart and your eyes. This story provides a vivid example of how to receive, and act on, angelic guidance and indication, so that you can live in harmony with the angelic sphere. When we consciously choose to live our lives this way, the human and angelic worlds can merge more fully.

In addition to Angels who appear on special occasions, there are certain Angelic Guides who are always with me wherever I go, including when I am at the university. These Angels are extremely beautiful and they assist me in my teaching, in my interactions with others, and in providing guidance and insight. Sometimes the details can seem quite mundane—such as reminding me to pick up something that I need at a store, or urging me to smile and make eye contact with someone, or presenting an alternative solution to a practical problem. All of their guidance is given to make life as happy and harmonious as possible. Very often, their indications are a source of great wisdom and joy.

One day I had to move from one building to another. Before I moved into my new office, the department chair graciously welcomed me and showed me several offices that were available, and he allowed me to take my choice. All of the offices were lovely, large open white spaces whose walls were lined with bookshelves, while a high cathedral window overlooked a lush canopy of live oak trees. As he and I stood together talking in one particular office, I looked up and, in my peripheral vision, I saw a very large Angel levitating between the high central window and the left-hand corner of the room. This Angel was extremely beautiful. Her energies were very feminine, and she appeared as flashing sparkles of golden and silver-white light.

Recognizing the Angel's presence with my physical eyes, I allowed the image to sharpen in my mind's eye and I saw that this Angel was carrying a garland draped over her two outstretched hands, the edges of which trailed over the sides of her dress. The garland appeared as a bouquet of etheric flowers composed of pink, white, and yellow roses, with some white lilies, baby's breath, and curling green ferns and sprigs mixed in between. As if this were not remarkable enough, I watched as this garland of etheric flowers turned into colored light, and then I saw it turn back into flowers. In my heart, I knew that I was being warmly welcomed into the new department, that I was being shown that I had a beautiful Angel accompanying me, and that the Angel was giving me indication regarding my choice of the office. Thrilled with what I was seeing, I sent this Angel love and gratitude, and I surrounded my words with bouquets of flowers.

Later on, I asked this Angel her name. She was quite embarrassed because, as I learned, she does not have a name; she has a title. She is called The Golden One, and she gives me protection, guidance, and indication. She is with me, always and in all ways. Both spellings are so important. Wherever I go, she goes, and there we go. This book is her book—and that of the many wonderful Angels who share my life—as much as the text is my own. Indeed, as I reflect on The Golden One's shifting garland of etheric flowers and colored lights, I can't help but think of how the Angelic Guides are assisting me in my writing. Very often, phrasings of words come to me that appear like little flowers strung together that attach to consciousness. The words form a thread that can be picked up and followed to carry us back to the flow of source. Returning to source means returning to where we all came from and melding with the Angels. As we follow this thread, the planet will become lighter because of this angelic melding, this returning to the light that we have never left, the light that has never left us.

### *Recognizing the Angels Who are with You Always*

1. Understand that there is an angelic sphere, and that Angels accompany you wherever you go.
2. Remember a time when you recognized a presence who is always with you, in good times and in bad, and with whom you have conversed. This is almost a mega-intuitive source or presence, one that is simultaneously deeply internalized and externalized. How does this presence appear to you? How does he or she make you feel?
3. Do you recognize this presence when you have a creative idea, or when you have to make a choice or decision? Do you have phrases of words or snippets of ideas that pop into your mind and flow together? Many people don't recognize this angelic source or use it to their advantage.
4. Give heartfelt thanks for the beautiful Angels who grace your life.
5. As you keep a journal of Angels, auras, and other spiritual experiences, you will be writing your own book of muse.

# 10

# Opening Up Your World: Angels at the Academic Fair

As you open your heart and your eyes, you will become more open to seeing the ways in which different types of knowledge and different forms of presence coexist in your life. This point bears repeating: In so many ways, the actual world that we all inhabit includes a strong metaphorical and metaphysical dimension, but we have to allow ourselves to see it. When you open yourself up to seeing the ways that worlds come together, more insight will become available to you, and you will know that you are always accompanied and guided.

At the beginning of the school year I volunteered for a shift at the Academic Fair that the university holds during Orientation Week, which is the week before classes start. In the large gymnasium, long tables were set up where each of the university's departments and centers had colorful brochures describing their programs, fliers listing the fall course offerings, the occasional tempting bowl of candy, and faculty members on hand ready to answer questions. The gym is a large, open space with polished wooden floors, and that day it was filled with bright natural sunlight, so it was a very inviting space for the fair.

As I sat at the Religious Studies table, I watched with great interest as the waves of incoming freshmen entered the gym. They were a diverse group that included a substantial international population, yet nearly all wore the colorful T-shirts that identified their residential colleges, as well as little round badges with their first names. Not only did the students come from a wide range of geographical locations, but they all had unique personalities. Some were shy and hesitant, while others were more confident and self-assured. During my two hour shift I spoke to scores of students, all of whom were extremely sweet and asked good questions.

When I attend events such as this, I always pay careful attention to how I feel immediately afterward. Are my spirits uplifted, or do I feel exhausted and wary? I have found that my own physical and intuitive responses are an excellent indicator of the tenor of a given situation. Both throughout the Academic Fair and later, as I was walking home, I felt a sense of excitement and buoyancy. A great deal of this can be attributed to the atmosphere that was created by the Angels who were present for the occasion. Throughout the fair I could see, feel, and sense that Angels were accompanying and guiding students to particular booths and tables, encouraging them to make contact not only with faculty in the fields they were expecting to study as major subjects, but to maintain an open mind and explore all the possibilities that the university had to offer. With joy, I could see that so many of the students were listening to their Angels, and this contributed to the atmosphere of buoyant lightness I felt all around me. The Angels pointed students toward certain tables and encouraged them to chat with the person who was advising on that particular subject. In turn, it was as if the Angels placed some of their own light onto the students, and the students shined with the hope, promise, and expectation of all they were seeing and the different types of knowledge they could be exposed to. It was so beautiful to watch, as the students and the Angels seemed to shine with one light, as the freshmen recognized just how much they could learn in the world that was opening up before their eyes.

## *Understanding How Angels Can Help You Learn New Things*

1. Know that there are Angels who specialize in education, and who assist with both teaching and learning. Call upon these Angels to help you with educational projects.

2. Recall the last time you felt that many new worlds and possibilities were opening up before your eyes. What were the circumstances? Was this experience connected to formal education, or to learning a new skill or hobby, or to discovering the treasures of classical film, music, literature, or art at your local library or museum? Recall how you felt as a new world opened up before you. Also recall if you were initially hesitant to get started, and whether you recognized that you were utilizing "angelic services" in your learning.
3. Put yourself in a position to learn new things. Maintain an open mind, and consciously allow yourself to explore areas that are unfamiliar to you, and to which you feel drawn. Does one particular area seem to stand out from the rest and even to glow? Work closely with your intuitive guidance.
4. Ask that you be angelically guided and accompanied as you enter this new world and absorb its knowledge. Give thanks for this opportunity for growth, for the discipline needed to practice in this area, and for the Angels who accompany you throughout your learning.

# 11

# Teaching and Inspiration: *The Bishop's Wife* and *Bell, Book, and Candle*

Among their many gifts, Angels are wonderful teachers. They are present in our lives to help us learn and to inspire us with new ideas. If you want to learn about a particular subject, or if you want to learn a new skill, you can always request that an Angel be sent to help enhance your knowledge. And if you are a teacher, you can ask that an Angel be present in your classroom to help you work with subtle energies.

At the university, I teach a seminar on "Life at the End of Life," which examines end of life issues from a range of interdisciplinary perspectives. When I last taught the class, several of the students were pre-meds, while others simply wanted to learn more about this important subject, and others still were openly confronting their own fears and grief issues. One of the early classes focused on the very challenging issue of biomedical perspectives on death. About halfway through the seminar, I had an in body/out of body experience. I saw myself teaching the class, commenting on the literature review, and taking questions about this difficult material. Yet I also noticed that another part of me had walked out of my body and was circulating around the room in spirit. I saw myself put my hand on the shoulder of a student who needed extra emotional support, while I took the hand of another student who was dealing with grief issues, and I whispered in yet another student's ear, encouraging him to contribute to the discussion. My spirit knew exactly where it needed to go during the class. As I have said, a mystic is a person who is able to be in multiple places at once.

On a lighter note, another course I teach is entitled "Show Me The Magic: Representations of Magic and Spirituality in

Modernist Cinema," a film seminar that combines my interests in religious studies and modernist visual culture. One day we were examining *The Bishop's Wife,* a charming Hollywood movie of 1947 directed by Henry Koster and starring Cary Grant, David Niven, and Loretta Young. Grant plays an Angel who comes in response to prayers for assistance and guidance from David Niven's character, a prominent Episcopal Bishop who is overwhelmed with work responsibilities. Chief among them is the cultivation of wealthy donors in an effort to raise money to build a grandiose cathedral. The Angel helps the Bishop to recognize his misplaced priorities of materialism in the construction of monuments to the ego. In turn, the Angel guides him to rediscover his love of his wife and the joy of living. In one notable scene, Grant's character makes an allusion to angelic claircognizance when he says that "Angels put ideas in people's heads," and then people think these ideas are their own.

Not surprisingly, the film inspired a lively class discussion. About an hour into our conversation, I looked up from my seat and I saw an extremely bright flash of sparkling, silver-white light. The light was hovering up high, near the ceiling. Below this electric-white light I saw three angelic forms. All three presences were very large and golden, and they appeared as loose silhouettes of energy rather than materializing more concretely and taking on personal appearances. These powerful angelic presences towered over the class, yet their energies were subtle, gentle, wise, and softly inspiring.

While a part of me was conducting a seminar discussion in real time with a group of fourteen undergraduates, another part of me silently thanked the Angels for being present. Without words, they told me that they had come to listen to the conversation that this group of young people would be having about Angels. And in part, they came to inspire the students with insights and ideas, just as Cary Grant's character does in the film. I couldn't stop smiling at the mirroring that was unfolding before my eyes, since a version of what we had just seen on the screen was now playing out in the classroom.

Before they left, the Angels told me that there would be a final reflexive turn later that evening as I described this scene in *The Angels In Between*. Indeed, the angelic realm is present in so many ways through gestures of mirroring and reflection that provide insight and inspiration. It all makes for a wonderful story, as Angels are indeed beings who give people ideas.

The story of Angels in the classroom doesn't end there. On another day, the class screened *Bell, Book, and Candle,* a Hollywood film of 1958 directed by Richard Quine, starring James Stewart and Kim Novak. This charming movie concerns the intersection of magic and love, the natural and the supernatural, and their resulting complications in American Cold War culture. While Stewart plays a conservative book publisher, Novak plays a glamorous witch who runs a New York gallery specializing in ethnographic and tribal art. Before the class began, I asked students to consider the ways in which a different type of "love triangle" was expressed in this work, one that concerned the conflict between 1). the edgy, transgressive, exoticized, outsider practices of magic and witchcraft, which were represented not only through spells and rituals, but through the African, Latin American, and Oceanic artworks displayed in the gallery; 2). the alluring visual cachet of style, fashion, and glamor in high modernist aesthetics; and 3). the expression of conservative bourgeois values, social norms, and cultural practices, particularly regarding class and gender roles. This was a wonderful, if challenging question, as I encouraged the students to think critically and imaginatively about the ways in which the conflict and the resonance between these themes worked together to create the tension and appeal of the film.

After we had screened the film and returned from a short break, I saw my students settling into their chairs and becoming extremely focused so that we could begin our conversation. As I initially went around the table and asked students for their responses, I saw with my physical eyes that Angels were standing behind the students, with their forms reaching up toward the ceiling. Yet I also saw that some very small Angels perched on the desktops in front of the students, where they had placed their texts and notes. These diminutive Angels were extremely beautiful. They appeared to be about six inches high, and their translucent forms were made of bright white and sparkling silver-blue light. I saw that both the large and the small Angels were guiding the students and helping them to formulate questions and express their ideas. In addition, the Angels were interested in the discussion concerning the intersection of various realms of being.

After twenty years of teaching at the university level, there is no question in my mind that Angels can—and do—enhance the learning experience in ways that we can only begin to imagine. On that particular afternoon, many different types of Angels were present as we sat together to consider the ongoing relationships between cinema and ritual in modernist culture. After the class ended, I asked the Angels why they so often put in an appearance in this particular seminar. With a twinkle, they smiled and told me, "We're showing you the magic."

### *How Angels Can Assist Teachers and Enhance the Learning Experience*

1. If you are a teacher, know that Angels are the teachers of teachers. Call upon the Angels of Education to fill you with inspiration so that you will recognize the magic and beauty of the subjects you teach. Ask the Angels to help maintain a high level of positive energy in the classroom, and to assist you in finding the clearest and most effective ways to communicate with your students.
2. Request that Angels be present in your classroom to guide

and enhance the learning experience and to inspire flashes of brilliance in your students. Be conscious of any creative insights that you or your students receive, and express gratitude.

3. Respect your students. Listen carefully to what they say and provide encouragement as they grow and expand. See the old soul wisdom shining in the eyes of their young faces.
4. Consider the ways that Angels may have assisted in your learning process, including inspiring your teachers.
5. Pay attention to how you teach yourself a new skill. Does your method of self-teaching seem to engage a subtle dialogue with unseen guidance?
6. Make a list of the ways that you learn (i.e. through books, through life experiences, through sensory impressions, etc.) and a list of the ways that you teach. Notice the correlations and the differences.

# 12

# Expanding into Beauty: Why Museums are Sacred Spaces

In so many ways, museums are workshops of ideas, creative spaces that allow human beings to see the beauty of what is possible. Museums can also help to teach the mystical ability of becoming attuned to the subtle layers of communication and energetic exchange that unfold both on and off the conscious levels. Sometimes this form of expression takes place through very subtle visual cues. Angels can assist you in discerning this special type of communication. As this chapter shows, it is possible to visit museums while conjoining your rational, intellectual knowledge with a mystical awareness that can guide you to personal and spiritual expansion.

As a historian of modern and contemporary art, I have literally spent thousands of hours working in museums. Much of my work has taken place behind the scenes, in archives and curatorial departments. And much of my work has taken place before the scenes, as it were, in front of original paintings and sculptures as I've lectured to groups of people in the galleries.

Spending so much time in museums, I've noticed something amazing. Museums are one of the few places (botanical gardens are another) where people truly open their heart as well as their eyes and allow themselves to look closely and see things that they have never seen before. This opening can be a powerful spiritual act, whether it is consciously recognized as such or not. In museum galleries, I have often seen people walking with their Angelic Guides close by. I have observed how the Angels act like flashlights to guide a person to a particular artwork that they will enjoy, or to use the piece as a teaching vehicle to bring light—both physical vision and metaphysical illumination—into a person's consciousness. If a particular artwork contains an idea or a lesson that is especially significant for you, the Angelic Guides can help to get your attention so that you will be drawn to the piece. When this happens, it is almost as if the Angels expand your mind to allow you to see more.

Sometimes when people pause in front of a particular painting, I can see that they have entered into a sacred pause. As they closely examine the surface of the canvas, they open their eyes wider to allow more of the scene to come through. Sometimes they step in closer to get a clearer view of the picture, and sometimes they step back in order to gain perspective and take in the scene in its totality. I have noticed that, as people pause before certain artworks and they open their eyes wider, they also open their minds to allow a broader view of life to emerge. And if an artwork is especially beautiful or moving, then people will open their hearts to the piece. This too can be a sacred expansion.

In these focused contemplative states, many people become aware of concepts they had never thought of before, or they may see or feel things that they could not have imagined. While these processes can be very subtle, sometimes as people open their eyes and their hearts, an opening forms between their conscious personalities and their souls. In these spaces between spaces, which unfold in the blink of an eye in the sacred pause before an artwork, a person can expand and meld with the beauty of the structure of thought itself. It always brings me such joy when I see people working with their subtle intelligence and their Angelic Guides in the museum gallery. Beauty, inspiration, and illumination are gifts because they open our hearts and expand our vision of all that is possible.

This sense that something beautiful is happening right now often occurs when I walk through a museum, and it also arises in my teaching, in my scholarly research, in my meditation, and in the work that I do at the hospital. This comes up when I work as a writer and an essay starts writing itself, as language comes to me very quickly with a particular phrasing of a string of words. Museums can be highly conducive to such flows of creative inspiration.

One morning I was visiting the Museum of Fine Arts, Houston with a colleague, and we were walking through a traveling exhibition of drawings by Rembrandt and his circle. At the very center of the first gallery was a small, gorgeous drawing by Rembrandt, the likely subject of which is the New Testament biblical story of Zacharias and the Angel. In this story, the Angel Gabriel tells the elderly Zacharias that he and his wife Elizabeth will have a son, who will be John the Baptist. While the iconographic attribution of the drawing is not conclusive, in this image a large Angel stands before an elderly man. The Angel's wings and hands are outstretched as he imparts news that the elderly man hears with rapt attention.

Viewed metaphorically, this story can be seen as a template for a human being's receiving news that something miraculous—and otherwise impossible—is about to take place. The image gives concrete form to the message that something beautiful is happening right now. As I gazed at the human and angelic forms and I recognized the broader message embedded in this delicate drawing, I knew that, at that very moment, something beautiful was happening at the museum, and that its wings just brushed against the corners of our world.

## *Visiting a Museum with Angelic Guidance*

1. Request that an Angel accompany you during a museum visit, then see if you are guided to visit a particular museum. This is a more advanced exercise, and you will want to practice seeing auras before and during the museum visit. As you walk through the galleries, know that you are viewing not only physical objects and their

visible appearances, but that you are also seeing the expressions of subtle energies embedded within physical forms. View the artworks both materially and metaphorically.

2. Maintain an open mind and an open heart as you take in unfamiliar sights and images. Allow yourself to be present with heightened attention and focused consciousness.
3. Knowing that your Angels walk beside you, see if you are guided to a particular work or exhibit. As you look closely, pay attention not only to what is visible on the surface, but to the feelings and energies that the work inspires and any intuitive impressions that you receive. Pause, and in your own mind ask any questions you may have about the piece. Then wait to see if you receive answers or ideas. This exercise is another form of reading multiple languages simultaneously.
4. See if you can discern angelic presences walking behind or beside other museum visitors, guiding them toward particular works.
5. Do you sense that something beautiful is happening as you visit the gallery? How does this make you feel?
6. Encourage others to visit museums as a novel way to see, think, and learn about the world.
7. As always, express gratitude to your Angels for serving as wonderful teachers and guides.

# 13

# Sharing Light and Exchanging Energies: Angels on the Skybridge

As we walk through our daily lives, we are constantly connecting with others as we exchange visible gestures and invisible energies. Through both modes of expression, we are continually sharing light. Such subtle communication is always complex and multiple, engaging so much more than meets the eye.

The Irish mystic Lorna Byrne has written several wonderful books, including a text entitled *Stairways to Heaven*. In this book, she vividly describes the experience of her soul traveling on luminous staircases that lead up to the heaven worlds, into divine and sacred realms. In turn, in my own life I have repeatedly been asked to practice the art of allowance, to consciously recognize angelic presences and accept their spiritual connections with the earthly world. While this has not always been easy, over the years I have found that these experiences have served as stairs leading me closer to the heaven worlds. The first time I saw auras while standing in line at the Post Office—and allowing myself to accept the reality of what I was seeing—was a step up to the stairway of heaven. Another set of steps concerns my practicing the art of recognition of the sometimes seen, and sometimes unseen, angelic presences who walk beside me, especially when I work at the hospital.

Because I take public transportation into the Texas Medical Center, the closest Metro Rail stop is located quite a long distance from the building where I see patients. It is about a twenty minute walk from the Metro to the ward, and much of this takes me through the Skybridge. The Skybridge is a suspended glass walkway that connects various parts of the widely spread out M. D. Anderson campus. At one point or another nearly everyone at the hospital travels on the Skybridge, including patients, caregivers, hospital visitors, and the medical and administrative staff. So when walking on the extensive Skybridge, scores of people are passing in lanes of traffic that move in two directions, both toward and away from you.

Recently, the Angels wanted me to try an experiment. First, they asked me to call to mind what it feels like when I'm walking on the Skybridge and I'm totally absorbed in my own private thoughts and not paying attention to anyone around me. Then the Angels asked me to consider doing things differently. They told me that they wanted me to walk the entire length of the Skybridge while consciously knowing, feeling, and sensing the invisible presences of the very large Angelic Guides who walk on either side of me. Before I started my trek, they wanted me to practice conscious attunement to feeling the presences of this unseen angelic accompaniment. While I wasn't allowed to see the Angelic Guides with my physical eyes, I was assured that these presences were very real, and very large and bright. So, off we all went together down the corridor.

As we walked, I was instructed to pay careful attention to how I felt differently in my own mind and body. And even more importantly, I was urged to pay special attention to how hundreds of people—of every age, gender, class, race, and ethnicity, and none of whom I had ever met before—responded to me. Thus the Angels were appealing to me as a scholar as well as a mystic, in order to make my experience more fulfilling. They were working with the comparative method, first showing me myself in a state of private self-absorption, and then asking me to contrast this picture with the conscious recognition of angelic presence. The results were dramatic.

As I walked, I noticed that many people tried to catch my eye and exchange a sweet and friendly smile. As I progressed down the glass corridor, I was allowed to see more. As people smiled at me, I literally saw a twinkle of light shining in their eyes. And then I was shown that, as I returned their smile and their twinkle, a beam of golden light was exchanged like a flash between us. This occurred nearly instantaneously, so in order for me to see this transaction more clearly, the Angelic Guides slowed time and increased the acuity of my vision. In that lucid state I could see that a beam or column of golden light sprang up from the eyes and briefly appeared to connect me to the other person, like a shared crown that extended between our foreheads.

Paradoxically, it felt as though, by expending this energy, each of us had more energy, in turn. I asked the Angelic Guides how this could be possible, and they gave me the metaphor of a car battery: as you drive a car, the battery becomes charged as the engine runs, whereas the same battery would become drained if the car sat idle in a garage and remained unused. While I am no auto mechanic, the Angels tell me that this metaphor provides a very clear way to think about how human beings can feel their energies being boosted and enhanced through rapid energetic exchanges such as this. In this vision of alternative energy sources, we all run on golden light.

This was such a great lesson for me. The reminder to connect with other people, and the allowance of what happens when I did, were all part of an experience where, as I walked the long, flat pathway of the glass Skybridge, I was also stepping up closer to the stairway of heaven.

### *Exchanging Subtle Energies with Others*

1. As always, know that energy is a complex living language that includes both visible and invisible components.
2. Ask that, as you perform this exercise, you are completely protected and guided.
3. Find an environment where you feel safe and where you will encounter people you have never met before. This could be a school, a hospital, a church, or a library.

Practice walking in this place in a self-absorbed way, lost in your own thoughts and showing no connection to others. How do you feel in this mode? How do you occupy your body physically? How do others respond to you?

4. Then walk through this same environment with care and conscious regard for those around you. Feel the Angels walking beside you and surrounding all people, and allow a quiet smile to form. As you walk, make contact with those around you. As you look briefly into their eyes, know that you are sharing a piece of your light. Can you feel the energy leave your physical being as it comes through your eyes as a gift to someone else? How does the person respond? Do they send energy back nearly instantaneously? How do their responses make you feel as you keep walking forward?
5. Afterwards be consciously aware of the circuitry of energy that connected so many different points of light. Do you feel that these exchanges empowered you and those around you, even if only in brief and subtle ways? Record your thoughts and observations in a journal.
6. Practice this exercise in at least two different locations in order to establish a comparative base of knowledge.

# 14

# Cleansing and Purification: Angels of Demanifestation

It is so important that we all cleanse ourselves, our spaces, and our spirits on a regular basis. As with all things, the Angels can assist in these acts of purification. The Angels suggest that you consciously throw away—or if possible, donate or recycle—something that you no longer need, and then pay careful attention to how your energies are lightened.

One day I was cleaning out my old office in preparation to move to another building. As I stood in one corner of the room discarding things, I saw that the recycling trashcan was becoming quite full. I was very happy about this move, and I reflected on how pleased I was to be demanifesting one environment so that I could transition to another. As I smiled and expressed my gratitude, I saw a brilliant flash of white light in the corner of my office where old catalogues had been stacked. In this act of cleaning, I was being assisted by an Angel of Demanifestation, an angelic guide force who helped me to uncreate one world so that I was free to create another.

There is great wisdom in the power of uncreation, of cleansing and demanifestation. In our contemporary world, we are all accustomed to accumulating, manifesting, and materializing our wants and desires. We are taught to do this from a very early age, and we are almost always rewarded for doing so. In general, we are not encouraged to uncreate, much less are we rewarded for demanifesting and clearing an environment so that we may have the regular cleansing and purification that create a pristine space.

These themes call to mind the alkahest, the universal solvent that was sought by the ancient alchemists. The resonant chain of associations is striking. Notice how the concept of "to solve" resonates with "to dissolve" and "to resolve." The solvent is the solution, the elusive fluid and the often equally elusive answer, the dissolution that is part of the solution in every sense of the word.

The wisdom and power of uncreation are often associated with the processes of cleansing and purification. While this may sound odd, I often see Angels in the bathroom. At first I was surprised and I wondered what was going on, so I asked the Angelic Guides why they so often appeared in the bathroom. While this may sound strange from a human perspective, the answer made total sense from an angelic point of view. Namely, the Angelic Guides told me that the water is conducive for them. Not only is water a conductor of electricity, but the bathroom is a space of cleansing and purification, where energy can travel and flow freely. The Angels tell me that, above all, running water cleanses and generates white light, which enables auric cleansing. (On a very practical note, hot Epsom salt baths are also wonderful to facilitate cleansing and purification.) Once you have had a certain number of such conversations, you begin to see the world in an entirely different light. Things make sense in a novel way because you are able to open both of your eyes simultaneously and see the world from a human and an angelic point of view. While human perspectives are often limited and flawed, angelic perspectives are of pure love and wild brilliance. What human beings can learn from the Angels is truly boundless. I wonder how many of us are ready for such boundlessness.

### *Receiving Angelic Assistance with Cleansing and Purification*

1. Recognize not only the practical value, but the spiritual significance, of cleansing both your physical environment and your personal thoughts and energies.
2. As you clean an environment, ask for angelic assistance

to give you extra physical and emotional stamina.

3. Throw away, donate, or recycle something that you no longer need. See how you feel after doing so—do you feel lighter and freer? Notice how additional space becomes available through this gesture. Consider how demanifesting one environment creates opportunities to manifest another.
4. Particularly at the beginning, start small, with a modest goal that you can easily accomplish. You can build up to larger tasks.
5. In advance, schedule a regular clean up time. Review and prioritize the areas that will be cleaned. Drink cool water throughout the cleaning. Record your feelings before and after the event. Begin to look forward to doing the same thing next time.
6. Consider cleaning up a personal bad habit. Ask that extra angelic assistance be provided to motivate and support you. Then, make it more difficult to do the thing you want to let go of, and conversely, easier to do the thing you want to do. For example, if you wish to practice a musical instrument, make sure it is visibly in your sight so that you don't have to spend time locating the instrument and getting it out of its case. If your goal is to increase exercise, have your exercise equipment and clothing in plain view and easily accessible. Know that you are communing with Angels who are dedicated to helping you accomplish your goal.
7. Consider whether cleaning up your present environment can help to provide a solution to a difficulty you may be experiencing. How can simplification or release of what you do not need help provide more energy, money, time, and space, both for yourself and your family?
8. This may sound eccentric, but if you are drawn to this exercise, you have nothing to lose. See if you are able to

discern Angels in the bathroom. As you shower or bathe, imagine not only that the dirt and the dust, but that the energies of the day are being cleansed and cleared, so that both your physical body and your spirit are refreshed. Consciously notice how you feel before and after your bath.

9. Express gratitude to all of the Angels who assist you in cleansing and purification, and who show you how the physical and etheric worlds are so deeply interconnected.

# 15

# Sheltering and Protection: The Angelic Umbrella

Just as you are always loved and accompanied, so too can you ask to be sheltered and protected by angelic light. All you need to do is to make the request sincerely.

One day I was on my way to work at the hospital, and it was very important that I was present to work with a particular group of patients and families. However, the problem was the weather. While Houston can go for long periods without any rain at all, when the frontal systems come in off the Gulf, the storms can be quite violent, with thunder and lightning, heavy winds and rain, and local flooding. That day threatened to be one of those days. As I took the first steps out of my backyard, I heard the loud thunder claps that corresponded to the dark red cells of the powerful storm system that I had seen earlier on the NOAA (National Oceanic and Atmospheric Administration) weather radar. Yet I needed to make my journey, and I needed to arrive safely. As always, I asked the Angelic Guides for help. As I walked out the back door they told me, "You like the rain. And you'll be alright, as long as you don't mind getting a little wet." I assured them that I didn't.

On the twenty minute walk between my house and the Metro Rail station, I passed under an extensive canopy of live oak trees. Although it was raining fairly heavily, as I walked I looked up and I saw that the uppermost leaves of the trees had spread out slightly so as to shoulder the falling raindrops. And then I noticed that, above the tree leaves, a trail of etheric angelic light followed me as I walked down the long, curving path of the boulevard. Much like the way the presence of an aura corresponds to the movements of a person's physical body, it appeared as though, as I walked, an umbrella of subtle light slightly preceded and followed me, shielding me from the falling rain. This trail of angelic light mirrored the small black umbrella that I held in my hands as I walked on the ground below, but it was much brighter and many times more powerful. While door to door it was a fifty minute trip by foot and light rail, I arrived only a little bit wet, just as the Angelic Guides had predicted.

This is another true story of shielding, protection, and accompaniment. Not only did the Angels respond to my request for accompaniment as I walked through the rain, but I was allowed to observe how they did this, and it was quite a vision. That day, the endless blessings of angelic tradecraft took the form of a moving canopy of light that surrounded and sheltered me. While the light acted as an angelic umbrella, I could just as easily say that an Angel's wing floated above my head while I walked on the ground below.

### *Requesting Angelic Assistance with Shelter and Protection*

1. Practice this exercise well before you actually need shelter and protection, and it will be easier during difficult moments such as storms. Ask that the Angels guide, protect, and accompany you throughout your journey.
2. Work with intuitive guidance as to how you should proceed. Listen carefully and see if you are guided to walk on certain paths rather than others, or whether you begin to notice features of the natural landscape or the urban environment that you might have overlooked. Understand the notion of "form meeting function," and look for angelic presences in the environment. Be willing to step away from the logical side of your brain that has already determined optimized routines, and see what lies behind the obvious. Even in retrospect, pay attention so

that you are better prepared next time.

3. Observe how some people are adept at doing seemingly complex things in a simple manner.
4. As always, express gratitude to the angelic realm.

# 16

# Accompaniment in Times of Crisis: The Hurricane and the Angelic Fireworks Display

Just as you are always accompanied, nowhere is this more the case than in times of crisis. If you ask, the Angels will do everything in their power to help you, and you will certainly not face the experience alone. This story will give you a clear and vivid image of what such angelic accompaniment can look like, and it also contains an intriguing suggestion for how to cleanse and restore peace after the traumatic experience has passed.

One of the most dramatic displays of angelic presence that I have ever witnessed—and I seriously hope that I never witness this again—came during the late summer of 2008 on the night when Hurricane Ike struck the Gulf Coast. Houston took a nearly direct hit by an extremely powerful Category 2 hurricane. We are fortunate to have a lovely old home situated on a high plot of ground. Even though our house did fairly well in the storm, the event was still traumatic. A huge old pecan tree in our neighbor's yard came within three inches of crashing into a plate glass door at the back of the house. Our fence and trellis were knocked over and there was debris everywhere. Most disturbing of all, the tall silver electrical pole that connects the house to the outside power line, and thus serves as the source of our incoming electricity, was ripped from the side of the house and hung dangling at a precarious angle, while the black power cord drooped low in our backyard. We were without electricity for twelve days during a cleanup period of extreme heat and humidity. Thank goodness, we never lost water. But for over a week I lived in terror that the power would come on suddenly, before I could get an electrician to repair the pole and reattach the electrical weatherhead, and that our house would burn down.

Without electricity and air conditioning, it was extremely difficult to sleep and I became exhausted and run down. To make matters worse, the university was already two weeks into the fall semester, and while the institution was proud that it maintained continuity in its class schedule, the experience was unbelievably hard on faculty and staff who were trying to repair substantial damage to their homes while, in some cases, being without electricity for nearly two weeks in oppressive heat and humidity. The physical and emotional drains were enormous, and it took me several months to recover.

Because this was the first major hurricane I had ever experienced, part of the fear was not knowing what to expect. The storm hit around 9 o'clock on a Friday night and we lost power immediately. One of the things I could never have imagined was the sound of violent rains and winds that gusted at over 110 miles per hour, and of this intensity going on for over twelve hours. I wasn't able to sleep that terrible night because I kept wondering if the roof would blow off, if trees would fall on us, and if glass would blow through the house and we would be forced to make an emergency evacuation. One of my primary thoughts was how quickly I could grab the cats and get them into their travel bags, and I kept both cats close beside me all night.

Okay, you get the picture. It was awful. All night I was half-sitting and half-lying in bed in the pitch black room in a state of terror. After a little while I noticed that, in addition to the lightning flashing violently outside, our bedroom and sitting room seemed to be filled with living energies. Bright patterns of colored lights were spinning and swirling everywhere. The electric colors ranged from bright emerald green to vivid blue, red, orange, white, and gold. These wild patterns were not the familiar, gentle sparkles of angelic forms that I was accustomed to seeing. Oh no. On this extraordinary night, our rooms were filled with what I can only describe as an angelic fireworks display of waving swirls, spirals, columns, ribbons, and fields of shifting colored light. As usual, the forms moved incredibly fast, and as if this were not remarkable enough, the two rooms were *packed to overflowing* with these energetic presences. I am not exaggerating. I have never seen anything like this before. There was so much electrical activity that I was afraid to get out of bed. It was absolutely incredible!

I later asked the Angelic Guides about what I had seen. I was told that, because the house was without electricity and everything was pitch dark, I could see the differentials far more clearly than usual. In addition, because the storm felt like an otherworldly event and I was so terrified, I was pulled off of my familiar moorings and I had entered a heightened realm of consciousness where I knew that potentially anything could happen. This dramatic disruption of my normative reference points jolted me beyond familiar boundaries and expectations, and this jolt threw me into a state of even greater allowance that enabled me "to see and accept more of what goes on every day anyway." (Can you believe that the Angelic Guides actually said this to me, namely that this type of thing goes on every day, anyway?) That night the immense power of the hurricane outside was met with equal intensity by an incredible fireworks display of vibrant angelic presences within.

After Hurricane Ike was over and our lives were returning to normal, I found that, in my mind, I could still hear the wind howling outside, and I still bore traces of terror inside. To remedy this situation the Angelic Guides made an extremely interesting suggestion. Namely, they instructed me to go through the house systematically and wash all of the mirrors and then place small quartz crystals in each corner of the rooms. By performing this ritual of purification, I was washing the external surfaces of the mirrors, yet I was cleansing the internal reflections that were still giving me nightmares. The grid of quartz crystals held the new pattern of cleansing and purification, both inside and out.

## *Recognizing Angelic Presences in Times of Crisis*

1. As with the previous exercise, it is best to practice feeling close to your Angelic Guides when you are not actually experiencing a crisis. This familiarity will make it easier when an emergency arises.
2. Know consciously that your Angels are with you always, especially in times of crisis. If you ask for their help, they will do all that they can, and you will not face the situation alone.
3. During a crisis, be aware of any unusual encounters or unexpected visitors, or of particularly dramatic displays of energy that might take you by surprise. As upsetting as this can be, when we are pulled out of our familiar patterns, our minds open more fully and we may be able to see things we have never seen before.
4. During an emergency, think about others—especially pets—who may be frightened, confused or otherwise picking up anxious energies from humans who are acting very differently than usual.
5. Angels can assist in long-term recovery. If you ask, they may provide practical steps to promote cleansing and purification. In the example I share, the Angels had me go through every room of the house and wash all of the mirrors systematically, a physical ritual that enabled me to perceive a different internal reflection. They also instructed me to place quartz crystals in the four corners of each room, to hold this new pattern of purification. This worked very well in restoring a sense of inner calm.
6. Consider any lessons that the crisis may have taught you regarding things that you can live without or that you do not need and consider demanifesting them. Does the crisis provide an opportunity for reevaluation or the chance to make a clean start on something?

7. Use the emergency to understand the functioning of other parts of you, which are not often used, and allow them to operate in the way they need to. We often find that we possess an innate wisdom that emerges during difficult times, and it is important not to get in your own way. One of the opportunities in the crisis might be the chance for greater self-awareness and recognition of areas that could benefit from reinforcement and improvement. Be sure you notice everything that you did right, and not just what went wrong.
8. Thank the Angels for all of their assistance, especially for the help they provided that you did not even realize they were giving you.

# 17

# Shielding: Angelic Protection from Dark Energies

Just as the angelic world assists us in times of crisis, so too do the Angels shield and protect us from dark energies. You can say a simple prayer that your life be protected by an unseen hand, and then express your heartfelt gratitude for this wonderful gift. This story not only provides a practical example of such angelic shielding, but it shows the extent to which angelic guidance can become so deeply internalized as to be intuitive. When you are living in harmony with the heaven world, the light is there even before you can ask for it.

At this point in my life, my connection with the angelic world is virtually automatic. My movements are in such close synchronicity with this sphere that I don't even have to think about them. This does not mean that I ever take the angelic sphere for granted. Not a single day passes that I don't express the deepest gratitude for the love and grace that flow through my life because of the Angels. One way to describe this relationship is that the knitting together of our worlds is so close and complete that it has formed a single, concordant pattern. In very practical terms, this means that I intuitively know where I am meant to be, where I need to sit or stand, what I need to do, when I need to say something, and when I need to sit in silence with someone.

Because this relationship is so close and immersive, it's only when things are "off" for some reason that I fully appreciate the extent to which my relationship with the angelic forces is always "on." At this point, there are two things that will routinely throw me off balance and disrupt the connection. One is my being in a state of physical exhaustion where I am overworked and over-tired. When my physical energy runs low, it's as though the electrical connection that unites me with the angelic world becomes frayed around the edges and the lights start to flicker on and off, as it were. The other factor that will sometimes arise concerns situations in which I know that I am meant to say or do something, but I will be shy or reluctant because of the energies of the other people around me. If I sense a great deal of hostility or resistance coming from someone in a room, or if the angelic world asks me to do something that seems a little eccentric (such as physically touching a particular object in a room for apparently no good reason, or humming a particular musical note in my throat), I will sometimes hesitate, even though I know I am meant to do this thing. All of my life I was brought up with very strict conceptions of etiquette and propriety, and sometimes these norms can be difficult to transgress, even though I find myself stepping over these conventions all the time. It can take great courage to walk in your own light, and sometimes I need extra angelic assistance to complete my tasks.

If I take a step back and look at the picture as a whole, I can see that the moments in the shadows are actually gifts because they provide a comparative framework that enables an even fuller view of life to emerge. Those instants of hesitation and embarrassment, or those moments of exhaustion, show me all the more clearly the ways in which the angelic connections are ever-present in my life. The metaphor that comes to mind is that it's a bit like living in a house where the lights are always on. You only really know the extent of the brightness when the power flickers and the room goes dark.

Because a nearly infinite number of details are associated with any given situation, it is often only when I review an event that I am able to recognize the extent of my interactions with the angelic sphere. For example, one day at the hospital I encountered a very young man who was very close to death from lung cancer. When the nurse first told me the patient's age, my heart went out to him and I decided to visit his room first. Yet from the moment I entered the room, it felt like I was trying to talk with someone from across a very great distance. The young man was fully awake, alert, and oriented, sitting up in bed and watching television. From the minute I introduced myself and looked into his eyes, it felt like I was trying to talk to someone who was at the bottom of a well, or someone who sat behind an extremely thick glass wall. I saw almost no light in this young man's eyes, his voice was monotone, and his facial expressions were very flat. And this only happens very rarely, but I could not connect with this man's spirit. I vividly recall standing in the hospital room being puzzled as to why I couldn't reach him. Our visit was brief and cordial, lasting about ten minutes. I knew I was not meant to be in that room any longer.

As it turned out, I saw several patients that day, and I ended up having a particularly busy week at school. So it wasn't until a few weeks later that I had an opportunity to reflect deeply on the encounter. As I sat in a contemplative state in the peace of my office, I was able to step back and see the picture more fully. This young man came from a very wealthy family, and the Angelic Guides showed me that he had something very dark within himself. This young man already had so much in life, yet a part of his character was insatiable and he wanted everything, including what other people had. Moreover, he felt entitled to taking what others had because he felt himself to be superior, and this was a great trespass and transgression. He entered into a powerful drug addiction that had, in part, resulted in this cancer. When people enter such states of severe addiction, they forget who they are. Now at the end of his life, these dark places were eclipsing the light of this man's soul. This was the reason why I couldn't see a path for moving forward while I stood visiting with him in his hospital room.

Once I was given this larger view of the situation, the Angels didn't need to show me the rest, as the pictures started flashing vividly in my mind's eye. I saw that the reason why I sensed such enormous distance between us, and why it felt like I was trying to communicate with this young man through a thick glass wall, was because the Angels had used their own luminous energies to form a dense transparent shield between him and myself. Thus, I actually *was* engaging with this man from across a far distance because the Angels had formed a wall of light buffering and protecting me so that no darkness could ever touch me. The Angels were so skillful, so instantaneous, and so seamless in their actions, and they were so modest about their efforts, that I was not even consciously aware of their gift until well after the fact. Only in the safety and distance of my own office did I recognize just how fully the beautiful Angels had my back, my front, and everything in between. As I entered that young man's room, I was completely encased in a living shield of angelic light. So yes, the lights are always on. But sometimes it is necessary to enter a darkened room in order to appreciate the full extent of the radiance.

The Angels are now asking me to tell you that the lights are always on in your life, as well. The Angels say that you can always request their assistance with shielding, protection, guidance, and accompaniment. If you are ever in a situation that feels uncomfortable or threatening, in your own mind and heart you can say a prayer and request that the Angels form a protective shield all around you. As they say, "that way, you can walk through your life knowing that you stand in the heart of the light." Afterwards, please remember to thank these beautiful beings who so readily came to your assistance. The Angels put their light on the line for us each time we ask them to do so.

### *Receiving Angelic Shielding from Dark Energies*

1. Regularly pray and ask that your Angels shield you from all dark energies and negative situations. Ask that your

life be protected by an unseen hand, and that the Angels form a shield all around you so that the heaven world accompanies you wherever you go.

2. Recognize people in your life who may have negative energy or be struggling with dark areas. Interact with great care, and observe the interactions carefully. If possible, build up your skills slowly and carefully. This needs to be practiced before encountering the dark energy of someone you have never met before, and who may be trying to deceive you. The familiar will give you a better sense of what to be alert for when encountering the unforeseen.
3. If you encounter a dark presence, immediately ask the angelic world for extra guidance and protection. Stand your ground and, from a position of strength, leave this presence as quickly as possible. If you have a strong feeling that you are not meant to go somewhere or talk to someone, respect your intuition and proceed with caution.
4. Be especially careful during times of physical or mental exhaustion, when your energies may be running low. Request additional angelic support during these trying periods. Do not overlook the roles of proper diet and healthy exercise in maintaining your strength and endurance.
5. Reflect deeply on everything that unfolds during a negative experience. In your review, pay attention to how this energy feels, how quickly you were able to recognize the pattern, and the ways in which you responded. For instance, were you intuitively guided to stand in a certain place, or walk with others rather than going somewhere alone?
6. Express heartfelt gratitude for how the Angels alert us to difficult situations, protect us when we are vulnerable,

advise us on how to protect ourselves, and guide us to safety. Again, thank the Angels for all that they do that you are not even consciously aware of, and ask for their help in increasing your consciousness.

# 18

# Silent Night: An Angelic Lullaby

The Angels tell me that angelic presence is a state of feeling as well as a state of being. While your mind must be open to the possibilities of love and the angelic world, you cannot think your way into a connection with this sphere through reasoning alone. In part, you have to allow the Angels to emerge in your presence, just as you must allow yourself to be present to them. The transitional state between sleeping and waking can be a powerful time to experience this sense of being present to one another. If you are having trouble sleeping, you might want to try this visualization.

One night at the end of the school term I found that I was completely exhausted, both physically and emotionally. I had finished the classroom teaching as well as the final push of grading. That week I also had to attend multiple faculty meetings and administrative meetings. To complicate matters further, the time between terms is really the only time that I can get very practical things done, such as auto repairs and attending to things around the house, and I had already started on these tasks, as well. As you can imagine, during that final week of the term I was in a state of total overload. Yet while I was so tired, I couldn't really relax, as my mind kept working on checklists of things to do—and even worse, I started to imagine more things that could break and require my attention. One night I woke up at four in the morning and I could not fall back asleep again.

After I lay tossing and turning for about fifteen minutes, I started to become upset, and I asked the Angels for help. I opened my heart to their presence, and they immediately responded. They told me to lie on my back with my eyes closed and pay careful attention to what they were about to show me. Immediately I saw a beautiful stream of clear sapphire blue light, like a flowing current or river. The stream appeared at the left side of my field of vision and flowed gently but rapidly downward toward the right. Then I saw a presence on the right, and it was trying to go in the opposite direction, from right to left, and it was struggling against the stream. I immediately recognized myself as this contrary energetic presence. The Angels told me to see myself jump into the stream of clear blue light and allow it to carry me forward in its flow. As if I were watching a movie, I saw myself leap into the light and ride the current.

Then I began to hear music, and the stream of sapphire light carried me straight into a lullaby. Very sweetly, I heard the words to "Silent Night." The Angels told me not to start thinking about all the familiar childhood associations of the Christmas carol, but to listen to the words as though I were hearing them for the first time, and to feel them in my heart as a sacred state of being. They told me to allow myself to merge and blend with the energy of the song:

*Silent Night,*
*Holy Night*
*All is calm,*
*All is bright*
*Round yon Virgin*
*Mother and Child*
*Holy Infant*
*So tender and mild*
*Sleep in heavenly peace*
*Sleep in heavenly peace*

It was as though I were experiencing the scene as a total state of being. I was in a sacred space filled with glowing stars and bright angelic presences. Just as the mother attended to her child, everything was in a state of perfect peace that surpassed all human understanding. Words alone do not do justice to the experience—it must be felt in the heart.

Lying in bed I became very calm, and I deeply understood that "Silent Night" is not just a familiar Christmas carol, but that it is also a lullaby, a prayer, and a sacred state of being. The Angels tell me that we can merge with the music and become one with the darkness and the light in a state of perfect balance.

### *Flowing with Angelic Presences*

1. Each day, consciously make yourself present to the Angels, even if only for a short time. As with any relationship, you must allow yourself to be present to them, so that they can be present to you.
2. This exercise may be easier to practice on days when you can wake up gradually instead of being jolted by an alarm clock. In the transitional state between sleeping and waking, imagine that you see a very bright wall of electric blue-white energy appearing at your left and flowing downward toward the right. Watch this wave of energy flow gracefully through your visual field. Then, imagine yourself approaching this flow from the right, and see yourself leap into the light. Allow the stream to carry you forward so that you flow as one, and see where the light takes you.
3. If you hear music, consider the ways in which songs can simultaneously function as lullabies, prayers, and sacred states of consciousness. Allow your energy to merge and blend with the total experience.
4. As you increasingly open your heart to angelic presences, thank them for their constant love and care, and send your love back to them, in turn.

19

# Expressing Gratitude: I'm All Yours, the New Normal

One of the most powerful things we can do is to express gratitude for all that we have been given in our lives. As you do this, your life will come into greater synchronicity with the angelic sphere, and you may begin to recognize gifts that you did not fully realize you had received.

Every day, as I walk through my life, I know that the Angelic Guides are constantly beside me, assisting me, illuminating me, and sharing their boundless love. Often I will see the Angels in the various ways I've described in this book, but some days they are less visible than others. While nearly every day I see shifting energy fields moving through space, sometimes it is more a case of sensing angelic presences and knowing that they are always there. While I am always thrilled and grateful to see the Angels, I also know that I don't necessarily have to see them to be aware of them. It's now a given that our lives are interwoven. Knowing this, and living it consciously, is the new normal.

When I wake up in the morning, I will often think about the day that lies ahead, and all of the work and challenges we will encounter. Then I'll smile and give thanks to the Angels who grace my life. Even before we begin, I'll express my gratitude for all of the ways that the Angels will fill the day with light, and thus, how they will make my life lighter in every sense of the word. Recognizing and acknowledging that we are making this journey together is the least that I can do, and it is the best that I can do.

Lying in bed, I'll smile and tell the Angels, "Thank you so much for all that we will do together. I'm all yours." And the Angels will smile sweetly as they reply, "Right back at you."

## *Understanding the Power of Gratitude*

1. Expressing gratitude is one of the most powerful yet underappreciated strategies for cultivating angelic connection and divine reciprocity. Gratitude represents a potent combination of recognition, humility, love, and mutual acknowledgement. Recognize the gifts you have been given and express heartfelt thanks.
2. Accept the Angels as a normal yet extraordinary part of your everyday life. As you walk through your day, know that you and the Angels are in it together.
3. Observe people who have a pattern of expressing gratitude, and those who do not. Do you discern fundamental differences between these groups? What are your own patterns of expressing gratitude (i.e. regularly, sporadically, or hardly ever)?
4. When you have received guidance in your life—including angelic guidance—do you tend to express gratitude to others and to the world at large, or do you feel that what you have accomplished is based solely on your own efforts and determination?
5. Periodically, look back on your life and reflect on people to whom you should express gratitude, such as someone who got you started on a career path, or who introduced you to your spouse. Do you feel that gratitude was expressed as fully as it should be, and in a timely manner? Is there anything you feel guided to do to bring things to balance?
6. Each morning, before you get out of bed, thank the Angels for all that they have done and for all that you will do together. As you express thanks, listen closely for a response. The Angels will return your energy, and you will want to be consciously present to catch the light that sails towards you.

# III

# How to Integrate the Angelic and Mystical Realms in Your Life

# 20

# Receiving the Gifts of Grace: The Archangel Haniel and the Arts of Allowance and Self-Overcoming

The Archangel Haniel teaches us how to practice the art of self-overcoming so that we may allow ourselves to receive the gifts of grace. Haniel is one of the most beautiful Angels I have ever seen, as her light appears as a splendor of opalescent and pearlescent radiance. As an Archangel she can be in all places at once, just as she embodies the capacity of white light to become all things. She teaches us that grace has three primary components, which she calls "a trinity of blessings." Grace relates to gifts and gift-giving, to freedom (gratis), and to gratitude. Haniel says that, within the hierarchy of Archangels, she stands beside, and on the side, of the beautiful angelic forces. She holds the grace that flows through all beings, and she holds creation as a tool. Through grace, she offers the energetic of creation. She tells me that she is delighted when the angelic forces take the grace from her hands to bestow to other beings. Haniel calls herself an Assistant for the Greater Good of the All. When the angelic forces use the grace that flows from her hands, this gives her exultation and reflects her strong need to serve. Part of the role of grace within the dynamic of creation relates to the cessation of fear. One image of grace is of a person being held in a supine position. Haniel says that, when you are receiving the gift of grace, it feels as though you are being completely enveloped in a divine embrace, held in closeness and held in love.

When we live in a state of grace, our lives align with the perfect patterns of the heaven world and we live by the light of our soul. We do not struggle against a situation and assert our individual wills, but we stand to one side, as Haniel does within the hierarchy, to allow the flow of grace to enter. To live by standing to one side of ourselves is to practice the arts of allowance and self-overcoming. This reflects the very beautiful mystical paradox of holding on by letting go.

Everyone is worthy of the gift of grace. To request the gift of grace, you can say a brief prayer, such as:

*Dear Haniel,*
*Please allow grace to enter my life as fully and freely as possible.*
*Thank you so much for allowing me to receive this beautiful gift.*
*Please help me to accept that white light can become all things,*
*So that my life can become a true reflection of the gift of divine grace.*
*Thank you so much for hearing my prayer.*
*Amen*

This channeled message is the view from above, from the realm of the Archangels. Now let me share some very practical stories that demonstrate the ways in which the arts of allowance and self-overcoming can manifest in our everyday lives.

Once a friend of mine was visiting Houston from the northeast, and he very much wanted to see a particular collection of paintings. While the works were relatively close by, the museum was too far to walk from my house, and the options for taking public transportation were very limited. So, we waited until an evening when the collection was open late and I drove us there. This friend had known me from New York and Boston, and in the big cities we always walked or took public transportation (or the occasional taxi). So, when we got into the car and I pulled out of the driveway, his first comment was, "Wow, it's a bit surprising that you ever learned to drive. For you, this involves such a great deal of self-overcoming."

I just smiled and told him to buckle his seatbelt, but his point was well taken. I have been driving since the age of sixteen, and

I am a good if cautious driver. However, by choice and inclination, I do minimal driving. While some people love cars and greatly enjoy driving, I do not and I never have. While I certainly appreciate having a car to carry heavy groceries or travel somewhere efficiently, I will always walk or take public transportation if at all possible. The bottom line is that, while I do not enjoy driving, my world is greatly expanded and enriched because I have this critical skill.

The art of self-overcoming is a delicate *and* a powerful subject. As human beings, we are constantly called upon to grow and expand beyond our familiar boundaries and established parameters. Sometimes this can entail taking on a challenge or learning a new skill. For me, driving represented such a challenge, as did developing the strength and balance necessary to do certain yoga poses that require a great deal of grounded energy. Yet these are worthy challenges, because they forced me to look at the parts of myself that needed extra strength and develop these areas in a targeted fashion.

One of the valuable lessons that I learned in yoga concerns how to allow the unseen world to support the physical body. Once I was attempting a modified version of a very challenging half-moon pose (*Ardha Chandrasana*), and I was having difficulty maintaining my balance. The class was performing this pose after more than an hour of rigorous practice, so we were all very warmed up, flexible, and focused. As I began to take the pose, I received the intuitive guidance to relax and allow the world to support me. In this deeply focused state of consciousness, I was told that I could perceive what appeared to be empty space as a kind of subtle energetic presence, and that I could imagine partnering with this space so that the angelic world was holding me gently and supporting me in the pose. This is a vivid example of practicing the mystical arts of allowance and self-overcoming to receive support from an unseen world. Can you imagine consciously partnering with your Angels so that your physical exercise practice becomes a spiritual one, as well?

As this suggests, a significant part of self-overcoming involves not struggling against yourself or a situation, but instead, practicing the art of allowance. Another lovely example I'll call "the light at my back." As anyone who knows me will tell you, I am not a morning person. However, sometimes it's necessary to wake up early. One morning I was presenting a paper at a medical conference, and I was one of the first speakers on the morning program. It was pitch black outside when my alarm clock went off, and I was groggy as I stumbled out of bed. One of my first thoughts was how much I hated getting up early, and an angelic voice clearly responded, "Don't struggle against it. Just flow with it." Because my eyes are sensitive to light and it was still dark outside, I stood at the bathroom sink brushing my teeth in total darkness, relying on touch to know where things were. As I stood there holding the toothbrush, I clearly saw a beautiful light appear gently at my back. An Angel was supporting me physically, indicating where things were, helping me to locate items, and going through the motions of brushing its teeth with me. Through this mimicking gesture, the Angel was providing an energetic template to guide my actions, and all I really needed to do was to follow its lead. Realizing what I was seeing, I immediately felt supported physically, emotionally, and spiritually, and I expressed my love and gratitude. Practicing the art of self-overcoming is so much easier when we can feel the light at our back and know that an Angel is standing right behind us, gracefully showing the way.

Sometimes the art of self-overcoming means having the capacity to get over ourselves so that we can see the bigger picture and be attentive to another. This takes skill as well as the conscious choice to open the heart and mind in order to see the world from another person's point of view. This often requires us to listen to angelic guidance, which asks us to be generous and stretch beyond our own needs, wants, and perspectives. When we do this, we are saying to the other person, without words, "I am making the choice to put you first, because you are the most important person in the room. What you have to say is the most important thing. You have my full attention." This type of focused presence is a gift of love and grace, and it is often associated with a very beautiful paradox. Namely, as we practice the art of self-overcoming and give our conscious attention to others, our world opens up in turn, and who we are expands well beyond the boundaries of who we had previously known ourselves to be.

### *Working with the Archangel Haniel to Receive Grace and Practice Self-Overcoming*

1. As Higher Beings, Archangels are especially large and magnificent Angels who are responsible for a particular area or sphere of being, and who work with legions of Angels to carry out their tasks and responsibilities. Call upon the Archangel Haniel to bring grace into your life. You can do this simply by making the request in your mind. Or, you can say the following prayer:

*Dear Haniel,*
*Please allow grace to enter my life as fully and freely as possible.*
*Thank you so much for allowing me to receive this beautiful gift.*
*Please help me to accept that white light can become all things,*
*So that my life can become a true reflection of the gift of divine grace.*
*Thank you so much for hearing my prayer.*
*Amen*

2. Grace relates to gifts and gift-giving, to freedom, and to gratitude. Consciously practice giving someone a gift with grace. The gift can be as small as doing a chore for them, or handing them a flower. You may find that gift-

giving becomes a regular routine. Each time someone gives you a gift, practice receiving it gracefully, with an open heart and genuine gratitude.

3. How does it feel when you handle a situation gracefully versus when you do not? How does an item look when it is created with grace versus when it is not? Observe closely how grace serves as a tool of creation.
4. Actively practice the art of self-overcoming. Learn a new skill, especially one that is out of your familiar patterns. Call upon Haniel and her angelic assistants for help, and observe how you are guided intuitively to do certain things. Try to smile as you learn. Request help with self-overcoming so that you do not take it personally when you make mistakes. Consciously know that you are practicing the art of allowance, and that such expansion allows more grace to enter your life.
5. Call on the Archangel Haniel the next time you need help with an unfamiliar or uncomfortable situation. For example, if you have to wake up early and you are feeling groggy, practice "leaning into the light." Imagine that an Angel of Grace stands directly behind you, supporting you and going through all the motions exactly as you do. Instead of struggling against the world, practice flowing with this angelic source, following its lead and moving gracefully.
6. Know when it is best not to struggle against a situation but to stand to one side and allow the storm to pass. When dealing with difficult people, try to open your eyes and your heart to the bigger picture, so that you become only a tiny speck in a much larger landscape. With this expanded vision, practice not taking anything personally and see if compassion and understanding arise.
7. If you are frightened, ask the Archangel Haniel for the gift of grace. Then, close your eyes and imagine being

held and cradled in a field of grace, completely enveloped in divine love.

8. Express your heartfelt thanks to Haniel for the grace she brings to your life, and ask that you be used as a tool to bring grace to others.

# 21

# Healing Old Patterns: the Archangel Raphael and the Angel of Inner Peace and Harmony

In many ways, healing old patterns represents an act of transformation that brings about internal cleansing as well as enhancing personal well-being and spiritual power. In this chapter the Archangel Raphael offers extremely clear, practical guidance on how to bring about internal healing, while the Angel of Inner Peace and Harmony shares his perspective on how to step beyond familiar boundaries in order to reconcile differences by seeing unity within apparent oppositions.

Despite all of the angelic assistance that graces my life, I am a human being and there are still times when I get worried. Sometimes it is necessary to be very strong and quell the mind. Through my teacher, the psychic medium Pat McKenna, the Archangel Raphael has spoken with me about how to turn a difficult situation around, and how to mend a broken perspective in order to heal an old pattern. The Archangel Raphael advises us that, when we reflect on a highly charged situation, time slows down in our minds. In the pause of the stillness, you can go within and ask yourself, "What is needed at this time to heal this situation?", and an answer will come very quickly. Raphael says that the rhythm of this healing process is: slow, slow, quick quick, like the foxtrot. Time slows down, and there is an acute awareness of a situation, and then there is the quick hit of instant guidance. To complete this dance you take that hit of insight, and you turn around and hand it back to the slowness of the situation to help bring about whatever change is needed.

One of the situations that we all face on a regular basis is going to the dentist, and for me, this can be a source of considerable anxiety. Of course, this is all about me, and it has nothing to do with my dentist and hygienist. Both are extremely kind, sensitive, and gentle practitioners who have been unbelievably patient and understanding, and I could not ask for better treatment. However, just the thought of having to sit in the dentist's chair can make me tense and anxious. The Angelic Guides say that those who are sensitive in one way can be sensitive in many ways, which is why I have such hyper-sensitivity to pain, both my own and that of other beings. Once I even found myself getting nervous the week before, as I was anticipating an upcoming dental visit. Because I truly desired inner peace, I sat quietly in a meditative state and I asked to connect with the Archangel of Peace and Harmony. Interestingly, when I first asked to connect with the Archangel of Peace, I was shown that I had to be more specific. There is an Archangel of Peace who works with external events and who aids in achieving peace in situations of war, conflict, and even family disputes. There is also an Angel of Inner Peace who assists individuals in achieving inner tranquility and harmony. This Angel says that you can call on its presence at any time to help achieve inner quiet, to assist in meditation, and to feel inner peace.

The vision I received was extremely interesting. The Angel of Inner Peace can give an appearance that is either male or female, depending on what will be most helpful and effective in a given situation. Because this Angel has the capacity to give the appearance of being male or female, this Angel *is* both male and female. The Angel is androgynous and incorporates diverse elements that can appear and manifest as differences, but which also exist in a state of harmonious union. This Angel is very powerful yet very calm and reassuring.

The Angel of Inner Peace and Harmony is also extraordinarily beautiful. This Angel appeared to me as a luminous green color, as if the color green were alive, alight, and on fire, while at the same time inspiring great peace, strength, and tranquility. The shades of green reflected another reconciliation of opposites, another androgynous union. The Angel noticed my fascination with the color of its appearance and he said to me: "A ribbon of green runs straight through the middle of life. This color sits at the center of the prism, at the heart of the light spectrum, and it can help you to find a middle pathway of peace." In particular, this Angel can show us what otherwise seemingly diverse elements have in common. This Angel teaches us about the multiplicity and the unity of our own natures, and how to make peace with ourselves. As she says, "Finding peace often involves locating a middle point of balance, so that you can reach a harmony that unifies the seemingly diverse parts and experiences of yourself. This is deep inner work that reaches out to the farthest corners of the self while holding everything in a loving embrace that goes right through the middle, straight through the heart. This embrace is peace itself, the intimate and ultimate gesture of love, self-love, and balance. You can go to this place when you sit quietly and look within. This will bring things back to center, because it is there that we find great harmony as well as the many fertile possibilities that resemble green shoots that promise the hope of new growth."

### *Working with the Archangel Raphael to Heal Old Patterns*

1. Call upon the Archangel Raphael when either you or someone you care for needs healing. When we reflect on a highly charged situation, the Archangel Raphael advises us to pay attention to how time slows down. In the pause of that stillness ask yourself, "What is needed at this time to heal this situation?" Take the first answer that comes, without critiquing the guidance. Take the instant hit of information, and turn it around and hand it back to the slowness of the situation. Raphael says that

the rhythm of this process is like the dance of the foxtrot: slow, slow, quick quick, slow, slow, quick quick. Thank Raphael for guiding you in this healing dance. Consider watching a video of the foxtrot, so that you will be familiar with the rhythm of the movements.

2. Know that Light Workers can be extremely sensitive to pain, both their own and other beings'. If you face a potentially painful situation, request angelic assistance. Practice being held by Haniel in a state of grace, and ask Raphael to guide the medical practitioners with whom you or your loved ones will be working. Know that you are not alone, and that you are attended by Angels. Pray that the Angel of Inner Peace accompanies you every step of the way.
3. Perceive the unity within apparent oppositions. Sometimes opposites are mirror images of one another. When reflecting on any extreme situation, consider the type of counter-energy that could bring the situation to balance. Ask that Raphael and the Angel of Inner Peace assist you in this process.
4. Give thanks to Raphael, to the Angel of Inner Peace, and to all of the Healing Angels in your life.

# 22

# Drawing on Intuitive Guidance to Make Strong Choices: The Line Down the Page

You can integrate intuitive guidance into your daily life in order to make strong choices and wise decisions. Sometimes this involves the art of self-overcoming. This chapter provides some very practical examples and a simple exercise that you can perform either physically or in your mind's eye when you are faced with a variety of choices.

My husband's birthday comes at the height of the summer, and recently his birthday fell during the middle of the week. By choice he and I share a car, so this means that I do not have access to a car during the daytime on weekdays. The day before his birthday was a Tuesday, and it was literally 102 degrees in Houston. In addition to having put in a very full day of work, I had exercised and I was feeling grimy. Moreover, by the time my husband came home, rush hour traffic was at its peak. So, I am ashamed to tell you the rationalizing train of thought that went through my mind: "Well, since tomorrow is his *actual* birthday, I can always pop out quickly tomorrow to pick up a birthday cake and some celebration things." This was immediately followed by the counter-thought, "Okay, but then when he comes in the door after a long day of work on his *actual* birthday, after spending all day in the office, he will not be greeted by the sight of a festive birthday celebration, and this will change the way he feels about his entire birthday." Thus even if it were a minor physical inconvenience, it was obvious to me what I needed to do, and which option was emotionally and spiritually the stronger choice. It was such a small thing, yet in my heart I knew how the consequences of both decisions would make my husband feel, and also, how they would make me feel. So I got in the car and I found a beautiful cake and some colorful streamers. The next day my husband's birthday was a joyous celebration.

Let me ratchet things up a notch. As I have mentioned, I truly dislike going to the dentist's, even for routine exams and cleanings. Yet I would dislike it far more if I did not go to the dentist's for routine exams and cleanings. Not only would there be physical effects, but just as importantly, the choice not to go would mean that I was putting myself behind a curtain of fear and apprehension. If I use my free will knowingly to live behind such a curtain of fear, then I am misusing my energies and I cannot be in my strongest and best form, physically, emotionally, or spiritually. So, twice a year I go to the dentist's for cleanings and exams. While I do not enjoy the experience, I cherish the sense of empowerment and well-being that come from making the choice to be in a position of strength. In this way, I am working with practical, intuitive, and spiritual guidance—and thus, I am working with the highest parts of myself—and not against them.

These examples are embarrassingly obvious, but the Angels urge me to share these stories because they make the point very effectively. The Guides say that the lesson is so deceptively simple that you may not think it's true. But it is. The bottom line is that, in most situations where we must choose between two options, we all know in our hearts and recognize in our minds which is the stronger choice. It's a little bit like the old cartoon character who has to choose between two options, and while he sits there thinking, a white Angel with a halo pops up on his right shoulder and encourages him to do one thing, and then a little red devil with a pointed tail and a pitchfork pops up on his left shoulder and urges him to do exactly the opposite. Indeed, one of the easiest ways to access internal guidance with clarity is to work comparatively and to feel the energies that attach to any given choice.

To make intuitive guidance concrete, you can approach the situation in a very practical way. The next time you are faced with two choices, get a blank sheet of paper and draw a vertical line down the middle. At the top of the left-hand column, write down the choice in positive terms, e.g. "Going to the Store the Day Before my Husband's Birthday" (or "Going to the Dentist", etc.). Opposite this, at the top of the right-hand column, write the alternative choice, e.g. "Not Going to the Store the Day Before my Husband's Birthday" (or "Not Going to the Dentist", etc.). Take your dominant hand and place it several inches over the sheet of paper, so that the vertical line runs directly down the center of your palm. Then place your hand over the left hand side and read the choice either aloud or silently, and see how this statement feels to you, energetically. When using your body as a divination tool, sometimes it is helpful to close your eyes so that you can focus exclusively on what you are feeling. See if you feel anything particular in your hand, such as whether this choice attracts you and pulls you in or repulses you and pushes you back. Pay attention to whether there is a great deal of energy invested in the choice one way or the other. Then go back to the center, shake your hand to clear off the previous energies, and follow the same procedure on the opposite side. It is likely that the two sides will feel quite different to you, and that you will have a strong sense of which is the better, more positive choice.

Making the stronger choice does not necessarily mean that this option will be easy or convenient. It takes effort to go out of your way for someone, including yourself. It takes energy to be generous emotionally, or to hold back a negative comment, or to stand up for someone who is being bullied. Yet this investment of energy will build your spiritual strength, because you are simultaneously practicing generosity to the spirit world, to others, and to yourself. As you cultivate your own intuition and openness to receiving internal guidance, and as you make strong, kind, and loving choices, in time these patterns become automatic. It is as though these choices become default settings. As this happens, a blending occurs between your conscious personality, the wisdom of your higher self, and the presence of your Angelic Guides. As practice becomes pattern, you move into a mode where you merge with the Angel within.

### *Using Intuitive Guidance to Make Strong Choices*

1. The next time you are faced with a given set of choices, ask the angelic realm for guidance. Sit quietly in a place where you will not be disturbed. Draw a vertical line down the center of a sheet of paper. At the top of the columns write each choice as a heading. Then close your eyes and place your dominant hand several inches above the center of the sheet. See how this middle position feels to you. Then place your dominant hand over the stronger choice and read it aloud or silently. See how this statement feels to you, both rationally and intuitively. Allow yourself to feel the choice and its consequences. Repeat this step on the opposite side.
2. Using your body as a divination tool, see if your hand is drawn to one choice or repelled by the other. See if your hand gravitates to one side of the sheet, or if one side feels warm and the other cold. Assess whether there is a great deal of energy associated with a choice, or whether the situation is more light and casual.
3. In your mind, consciously practice making the weaker choice. Reflect on both its short-term and long-term consequences. How do they differ? Even more importantly, how are you a different person internally because you made this choice? Think back to a time when you made a weaker choice and reflect on the impact of that decision.
4. Then consciously practice making the stronger choice.

Again, note how things unfold differently both in the short and longer term, and how you feel differently because you made the stronger choice. Work comparatively so that subtle energies register clearly in your conscious mind.

5. Especially if the stronger choice is the more difficult choice, know that you are practicing the arts of allowance and self-overcoming, and thus, you are working with the Angels of Grace. Ask Haniel to assist you, and thank her for allowing the flow of grace to enter your life.
6. Practice this exercise on a regular basis so that making stronger choices becomes your default setting. Work consciously with your intuitive guidance to merge with the Angel within.

# 23

# Listening to, and Acting on, Angelic Guidance: The Colored Pencils

All people can potentially serve as our spiritual teachers. When you listen to, and act on, divine guidance, not only do you have the ability to bring joy and comfort into people's lives, but you receive the gift of allowing the angelic world to become integrated even more fully into your own life, as well.

One afternoon I was preparing to leave the hospital after having put in a very full day on the ward. As I walked down the long corridor toward the elevators, I glanced into the family room and noticed four small boys sitting quietly in the corner. They ranged in age from about five to ten, and they were all very good children, reading, listening to music, and playing quietly with their handheld devices. The boys were supervised by a pretty young woman who sat on a sofa at the opposite end of the room. A short distance away, on the palliative care ward, one of their elderly family members lay very close to death. The boys seemed untroubled by what was occurring, and everything appeared to be in good order, so I kept walking.

Just before I reached the bank of elevators, an Angel urged me to turn back and share the handmade paper journals and colored pencils in my bag with the boys. The journals and pencils are not toys to entertain children; rather, they are the tools I use to produce end of life narratives. However, in a flash of intelligence, the Angel who attended this group showed me that this family was very private about end of life issues. The boys had not been told the entire truth of what was occurring, yet the children knew that the situation was gravely serious, and they were both frightened and very sensitive to the grief and sadness they felt all around them. The children played so quietly because they were under an emotional strain. Receiving an unexpected gift would bring them much-needed happiness. In short, the Angel was urging me to open my heart and my eyes so that I could practice the art of self-overcoming, see the bigger picture, and act on it sweetly and swiftly.

I immediately turned back and walked into the family room. Speaking very quietly, I approached the young woman and asked if the boys were with her. She said yes, they were, and then I introduced myself and offered the art supplies for the children. Across the room, the littlest boy was listening eagerly to our conversation. As we spoke, he gradually drew closer. He was already at arm's length and listening attentively when he heard the young woman say yes, the boys would be happy to receive the art materials. When I handed her the journals and colored pencils, the light in this child's eyes and the joy in his smile were absolutely radiant, and I could feel my own heart glowing, in turn. That afternoon the little boy and his family's Angel were my teachers, imparting to me valuable lessons of light, love, and generosity.

I know that everyone reading this book has experienced a version of this situation. While this story is such a small thing, it is a very clear and concrete example of listening to, and acting on, angelic guidance. One of the keys to knowing angelic presence is to practice generosity, and this always begins with conscious attention. Giving conscious regard to the angelic world creates the conditions that enable us to feel the Guides' presences and respond freely. Emotional generosity precedes material generosity, and conscious attention precedes all else.

### *Listening to, and Acting on, Angelic Guidance*

1. Recognize that spiritual lessons can arise anywhere, and that all people can serve as our teachers.
2. Practice a pattern of conscious attention, emotional

awareness, and physical action. Seek opportunities to bring joy or comfort into someone's life. These can include making a donation to a philanthropy, smiling at someone unexpectedly, making a small gesture of kindness, or giving someone an unexpected gift. Have no expectations about the person's response and remain open to whatever arises.

3. Recall past experiences where you made an effort to help someone, or provide joy, and it was not received well. Did this experience keep you from making such an effort again? Understand that not every gift meets with an expected response, and thus, release any expectations.
4. Be aware of people who need your help and do what you can to assist them and bring light into otherwise dark places. Know that your Angels are working with you closely, and ask that the other person's Angels be brought in to reinforce the light.

# 24

# Accepting What We Cannot Know: Ghost Writers

A substantial part of practicing the arts of allowance and self-overcoming concerns various types of surrender. One familiar situation is when we ask a question and an answer is not readily forthcoming. As human beings, we can only receive—and thus, we can only give—what we're given. So it's important to know how to respond gracefully when we do not receive information, and how to accept what we cannot know.

Very often, when I am sitting quietly in meditation or when I am working with people, I will get flashes of insight and information. Sometimes they arise spontaneously, and sometimes they come in response to a specific question or discussion I'm having with the person. Sometimes I receive only partial answers, and often I am shown what appears to be related metaphorical imagery. On some occasions I don't get any information at all. It is impossible to predict what will, or will not, come forth during a given encounter. When I am working with someone, I can only give as much as I am given. I can only give what I receive.

I have asked the Angelic Guides about this, and they tell me that the stories behind many people's questions can be infinitely complex and expansive. Sometimes the stories have yet to be fully written, and they can involve the lives of multiple people. The Angels show me that people's life stories are like novels. The stories can fill tens of thousands of pages, and yet there will always be more than anyone can ever know. On these subjects, the Guides tell us:

"When we give you information, it is because that is what can be revealed at the time. We will only give as much information as the person can absorb and integrate, and we will present it in the language that will be most useful and meaningful. Doing energy work together, and experiencing an angelic encounter, can feel overwhelming for some people, especially if they are not accustomed to such experiences and the openings and transformations that can follow. This is why we use familiar metaphorical images that will be clearest to the person and of the greatest value. These are the images that will stay in a person's heart.

"Trust the process. Trust what is given, and trust the silence as well. Great silence can be both eloquent and elegant. When an answer is not readily forthcoming, it is not because we didn't hear you. We are not away eating lunch at a new restaurant, and we are not not answering your calls because we are taking a break from you! Instead, we want you to think of these pauses like the silences that form music, or the dark spaces that create the action that takes place off the scene in a play. These spaces of silence are like the ellipses in a poem, the pauses in language that are filled with so much potential, just as you are. We are always here to help you, although we are sometimes seen, and sometimes not. Sometimes we give silently, as we work together like 'ghost writers' on a novel that we are all writing together, a magnificent collaborative project, we assure you."

## *Accepting the Unknown*

1. Recognize that there will be times when you must accept the unknown. When you ask a question and no answer is readily forthcoming, try to surrender to the silence as gracefully as possible rather than struggling or attempting to force an answer.
2. Regardless of the information that comes forth, know that there is always much more to a situation than meets the eye. Also recognize that everyone has free will, and sometimes people do not wish to receive guidance. This is

their choice and it must be honored.

3. Practice being in a public space and not being able to hear, such as by using earplugs. Learn to observe the unspoken part of the world and the various non-audio cues that abound.
4. Know that sometimes unknowns are not really unknown, but that it may not be worth the trade-off to have this information at this time.
5. Know that your prayers are always heard, and that your Angels always love you and will never leave you. This is simply not possible. Yet when engaging the angelic realms, we are often dealing with mysteries that lie well beyond human comprehension. Hold this broader vision and accept it with humility. Trust the words that arise, and trust the silence equally.
6. As always, express your gratitude for all the guidance and accompaniment your Angels provide, whether you are consciously aware of these gifts or not.

# 25

# Seeing the Links between Humor, Metaphor, and Mysticism: "Don't Call it a Fruitcake"

Just as metaphor can be a powerful vehicle for conveying multiple meanings simultaneously, so too can humor. Both humor and metaphor are game changers, as they can allow you to be in many places at once.

Two days after I started writing this book, in my mind's eye I kept seeing the most incredible desserts floating all around me. It was like I was being given a private tour of the bakeries in the Halls of the Heavens. Above all, I kept seeing a particular piece of pastry with a hyper-intense clarity. This elaborately decorated dessert looked like a cross between a fruitcake, a strudel, and a Danish pastry. The heavenly golden bread was twisted into a semi-circular shape that resembled a wreath. Inside the sweet buttery bread were brightly colored candied fruits and nuts. The exotic fruits were golden yellow, ruby red, and bright emerald green, and they all resembled jewels that glowed with an intense inner light. A light coating of white frosting appeared like gentle snow on the glazed surface of the pastry.

I am not a cook, so I cannot tell you exactly how to create this dessert, but I am being shown that, in addition to these elements, the pastry also contains cinnamon, pecans, and raisins. The Angels tell me that there is brandy in the recipe, and that "the alcohol will evaporate during the baking process but the raisins will absorb the flavor of the spirit, and so will you." As I type these words, the Angelic Guides are laughing a little at the charm of their own metaphor.

Because this pastry kept appearing before my eyes, I asked the Guides about the meaning of the symbol. They responded that this dessert is a metaphor of creation for *The Angels In Between*. The Angels say that the writing in this book is very sweet, especially in the intimate atmosphere and warmth of the discussions, and that I have words and images that glow like jewels on the page. The metaphors will gently feed people's spirits, as if they are eating the most heavenly pastry.

Hearing this, I thought to myself, "Great, just great. So now I'm working on the literary equivalent of a fruitcake, and this is a symbol of my spiritual memoir. I can just imagine the jokes that will come out of this."

The Guides smiled and reassured me that, while some people could respond that way, my own sweet readers will not. Instead, they will love this creative imagery and the experience of savoring a story that is seasoned with spirits.

Over the years, I have noticed that the Angels have a special fondness for plays on words. Even as they smile, they tell me that there is a serious purpose to this. The Angels say that humor provides a gentle and effective way for human beings to recapture the magical ability to see the same thing in a completely different way, or to see two seemingly different things in a similar way. It's like a ball that bounces back and forth between two children, with the same ball doubling back and forth as the children pass it between them. The Angelic Guides tell me that humor is a way to keep our spiritual muscles in shape so that we can move gracefully between multiple meanings, so that we can balance multiple perspectives at once. Again, one of the definitions of a mystic is a person who is able to occupy multiple locations simultaneously.

The Guides also say that the pastry metaphor, which combines many layers and ingredients, teaches an important lesson about the lightness and multiplicity of being. It all depends on how you look, and what you are looking for, as to how the world will look to you. The amount of openness that you allow will shape the appearance that the world takes on before your eyes.

As I write these words, I can see the pastry floating before my eyes. Looking at this with me, the Angels are cocking their heads to one side and saying with a smile: *"Don't call it a fruitcake, my dear. Call it a metaphor of allowance and becoming, and invite your readers to savor the sweetness of the Total Creation."*

### *Recognizing the Links between Humor, Metaphor, and Mysticism*

1. Recognize that humor, like mysticism, often engages a play of multiple meanings. Notice jokes that feature plays on words, and observe how humor represents a distinctive form of creation. Just as you did with dream analysis, reflect on the ways in which a single object can hold multiple meanings at once.
2. Observe how humor can transform a situation. Notice how humor allows you to see the same subject in multiple ways, or two different subjects in a similar way. When you laugh, think of humor as a tool to keep your spiritual muscles in shape.
3. Notice how you feel before you start laughing. Then watch a film or program that is particularly funny, and reflect on how you feel immediately afterward. Do you feel freer after a good laugh? Like spirituality, humor engages a lightness of being, a levity that can give you a sense of levitation, of flying free.
4. Take time to understand how humor works in other cultures, and the types of things that people find funny, and what they do not. Pay particular attention to the difference between humorous words, actions, and scenarios.
5. Remind someone after the fact that they were funny and enjoy recalling the joke or situation together.

6. Observe carefully the ways in which humor can have a dark side, which can take the form of jokes at the expense of others, a gesture that diminishes another person's power. Again, notice the energetic relationship between humor and the power of creation, either for light or dark purposes.

# 26

# Using Humor to Transform Situations: The Bouncing Beach Ball

Angels have a terrific sense of humor. They are experts at showing us how humor and play, including playing with words and energetic variables, can dramatically alter a situation. By transforming our attitudes, humor can enhance our personal power.

After the encounter with the golden eagle in Arizona and the lucid dream of the islands in the sky, I noticed something very interesting. As I walked through my everyday life, my physical eyes and my spirit eyes merged, and I could consciously shift between different modes of vision. Both then and now, there are times when it is necessary for me to stay grounded and anchored in the physical world, and then there are times when I am walking in mixed psychic terrain, as it were. Sometimes when I am supposed to stay present in the mundane world, I become bored and my spirit starts to wander. It is at these times that I know that the Angels definitely have a sense of humor. The Angelic Guides know that I bristle spiritually when I'm engaging energies that are very weighty and formal, either socially or professionally. Alas, this is particularly the case when I find myself surrounded by figures of power and authority. At these times, the Angels will often entertain me in a variety of ingenious ways. It can be very difficult not to laugh out loud, especially when it is *not* appropriate to do so.

One day I was standing in the marble corridor of the main hallway of a very old and prestigious college. I was waiting for a colleague, and I had to wait for quite a long time. The President's Office was situated at the center of this long hallway, and on either side were the offices of the senior administration. You couldn't turn around without seeing a Vice President, and there were several. The marble corridor had heavy sections of dark oak paneling hung with portraits of past university presidents, trustees, and other dignitaries and benefactors. In short, this was a corridor of power. The atmosphere was very quiet, heavy, formal, and austere, and I did *not* feel particularly comfortable standing at the end of this long hallway that seemed to stretch on forever. I remember wondering, "Where the hell is my friend, and what on earth could she possibly be doing all this time?"

As I stood contemplating the portraits, one of my Angelic Guides called out to get my attention. The Angel was standing several feet in front of me, a bit deeper into the hallway than where I stood at the outer edge. Then I noticed that this Angel was holding what appeared to be an extremely large and colorful plastic beach ball. The multicolored beach ball had swirling sections of red, white, blue, yellow, and orange, and it looked exactly like the type of toy that my sister and I played with at the beach when we were children. This Angelic Guide smiled at my obvious surprise as I telegraphed the thought, "Oh my goodness, what are you doing now? Can't you see where I'm standing?" With a smile like a star he twinkled and replied, "Oh yes, we see *exactly* where you are standing. That's why we're sending you this. Catch!" And then he threw the light, etheric beach ball down the corridor toward me and started laughing gently.

A part of me was absolutely mortified. I mean, *what if anyone could actually see this?!* And then I realized the ludicrousness of this thought. If anyone else were clairvoyant and *could* actually see this, the odds were excellent that they would want to play with the beach ball, too. So I smiled, and I tossed the ball back to the Angel. The Angel caught it and then he disappeared, yet he kept the image of the beach ball bouncing before my eyes, more vividly than ever, as he threw the ball back to me again and laughed. Please keep in mind that, when this happened, I was an adult in my early thirties. Yet the Angel ingeniously found a way to entertain me and take the serious edge off of the dense, stuffy atmosphere of power that filled the corridor. Then, best of all, the Angel invited me to be irreverent. He handed me the colorful beach ball and encouraged me to throw it down the corridor and watch it bounce. I hesitated for a moment as again, I thought to myself: *but what if we got caught?* Then I let it fly. With great satisfaction, I watched the beach ball bounce up and down on the black and white marble floor. It nearly touched the ceiling before it came back to the ground, skipping happily down the corridor of power. So for a little while, Professor Brennan stood there playing bounce and catch with the invisible angelic presence who was my playmate.

Then the scene returned to normal. My friend appeared, and it was time for us to go on with our day. Yet as I did so, I could feel that, as I walked, I carried traces of bouncing colored light and sparkling angelic magic. This shimmering lightness of being followed me, almost imperceptibly, as I walked down that long corridor of power. Now, *You Catch!*

### *Using Humor to Transform Situations*

1. The Angels know that creation comes from joy, and they are accomplished mimics and comedians. The next time you find yourself in a particularly formal environment, sit quietly and see if you can discern angelic presences. Allow your physical eyes and your spirit eyes to merge, just as you do when seeing auras.
2. Particularly if you find yourself in a stuffy atmosphere, ask your Angel to lighten the situation. Then, try imagining this same scene from an angelic point of view. What has shifted, and how does the world appear differently? Notice how humor brings lightness to heavy environments. Do you sense that unbalanced energies are in greater balance, and that you feel more powerful as a result?

3. Actively seek out a stuffy environment and sit quietly in this space. Observe how people behave and interact with those around them. Look for any traces of humor in these places and pay attention to their source. Then, visit an environment that is more casual, such as a grocery store, and repeat this exercise.
4. As always, thank the Angels for the wisdom of their humor and lightness of being.

# 27

# Recognizing the Facts of the Matter versus the Stories We Tell Ourselves: Showing Up at Our Own Parties

We have all been in situations where we have had to stop denying the truth and telling ourselves stories that cover up inconvenient, and sometimes painful, realities. The bottom line is that we cannot lie to ourselves or to the spirit world. When we do not honor the truth and we choose to live in a state of denial, we can become very ill, both physically and spiritually. As always, angelic guidance and protection are available during these challenging times. These stories represent a radical example of the need to practice the arts of allowance and self-overcoming, and what can happen when we do not. When we allow ourselves to recognize the difference between the facts of the matter versus the stories we tell ourselves, we truly start living our lives and showing up at our own parties.

One afternoon I was sitting on the couch, drinking coffee and watching one of my favorite old films. As I looked up, I saw two Angelic Guides standing directly in front of me. As always, they were so luminous, so kind and beautiful, yet it was clear that they had a message for me and that they meant business. I suspect that the heaven world sent two for reinforcement purposes, just to make sure I got the picture. The female Angelic Guide on my left held a tall rectangular book in her arms, while the male Angel on the right held what looked like a quill pen with a golden nib and a pot of golden ink. In a single voice they said, "You know that you have to tell *that* story."

This is a story that I never wanted to write, and heaven knows that I never want to live through this again, either. This happened several years ago, and now I am in a very different place than when this story begins, so it is safe for me to describe the situation. The Guides tell me that, while this particular story relates to academia, "These types of behaviors go on everywhere. These power dynamics can arise in any situation. It can be a medical practice, a law firm, a corporation, a small business, or even a family. These things happen in any place where human beings have power over one another."

There are things that go on in life that we suspect, even though we don't want to believe that they are true. Quieting the mind enables us to discern the truth, which is the difference between the facts of the matter versus the stories of denial we tell ourselves. Both the body and the soul are infinitely wise, and they know things that sometimes we have trouble admitting to ourselves, because these realizations seem to be too difficult, inconvenient, or unpleasant to face. Here is the story that I didn't want to tell:

Exactly one year after I started my tenure track job at the university, I became very ill. I developed a crippling, painful case of gastritis that was crystallizing into an ulcer in my intestinal tract. Not only was this experience physically painful, but it was emotionally terrifying. The hardest parts were the nights. There was one stretch where, for three months, I couldn't sleep and I actually lay in bed wondering if I were going to die. A part of me simply could not understand why this was happening. Yet another part of me knew very well, and I refused to acknowledge this voice. The bottom line was that I truly *was* in a very difficult situation. I was in a high-pressure professional environment that was physically exhausting, and we were overloaded with work. Part of the reason for this unnecessarily demanding workload was that ambitious people in senior positions off-loaded a lot of time-consuming, demanding, and thankless service tasks to junior people who were not in a position to refuse. This had nothing to do with teaching or scholarship, and this reality was so different from the ideals that I always held about academic life. In short, the gap between the facts of the matter and the story that I told myself was so enormous that I simply could not cross it. So, instead of acknowledging the reality that was unfolding all around me—let alone owning up to how I actually felt about it—I went into a state of denial, and I kept telling myself, "No, that can't be true."

The Angelic Guides tried to show me difficult things that I needed to see, for my own knowledge and protection, and I kept shutting them out. Regarding my continual denial and my tacit anger and sadness in refusing to accept the situation, the Guides finally told me, "We do not want to hold your garbage any longer." So, through both my claircognizant and my clairsentient channels, the Angels would warn me, "Don't express that thought aloud. It's a splendid idea, and the person you're talking to will steal the idea and claim it as their own." To which I responded internally, "No, that just can't be true. They wouldn't do that!" This went on as a kind of constantly running internal dialogue. The Guides would say, "Watch closely now, because that person will say one thing publicly and do another thing the moment he is alone in his office. He will feel completely entitled in doing so, and he will take delight in his exercise of power." And I immediately responded, "Wow, that's really disgusting and dishonest. No! That just can't be true." Another time, the Angelic Guides nearly suspended time during a lunch meeting so that I could recognize what was happening and respond accordingly. I felt the Angels hovering somewhere between the top of my head and my right ear. They slowed everything down and they said to me, "Right now the person you're talking to is flattering you because they are going to try to manipulate you, because they want to use one of your publishing connections." And of course, it happened exactly as they said, just a moment later.

Another time, the lesson was retrospective, and the Angelic Guides made their appearance a split second after an interaction had occurred. This example took place at a holiday party at a colleague's house. A prominent person walked from the living room into the kitchen to get a glass of wine. I smiled and said hello as she looked around for a wineglass. She barely acknowledged me and she never made eye contact. A few minutes later, the hostess of the party introduced us, and this woman's attitude changed dramatically when she heard my name and title. Perhaps it's naïve, but I was completely appalled. Just to make certain that I learned the lesson so that it made a lasting impression, the Angelic Guides popped in and said, "Just notice how this person treated you one way when she didn't know who you were, and this was because you had a quiet demeanor and she thought you were 'a nobody.' Then, just look at how her attitudes shifted when you were introduced and she recognized that you are 'a somebody.' A powerful colleague in New York had told her to watch out for you, and now she's gratified because she has made this contact socially and she can go back and tell her friend." This was followed by an immediate reaction of revulsion inside of me: "Yuck, this is just awful! So petty! It's a holiday party, for heaven's sake, and can't we just give this a break this one evening?" Of course we could not "just give this a break" because it went on all the time all around me, and it was all too true.

I won't give any more examples, as the pattern is clear. Yet as unpleasant as this is, there are important lessons in these stories. The first lesson has to do with the issue that we all speak multiple languages simultaneously. There is the language that people speak openly in words, and then there is a second, subtle language of energy that unfolds behind and beyond the first language, and this language resonates well beyond the words that are spoken aloud. Sometimes the messages of the two languages are in accordance, and sometimes they are not. The dissonance is the distance between these two spaces, and it is like a negative crack of opacity, egoic self-interest, obstruction, hiding, and lies. It's very unpleasant. The Angelic Guides also point out that some people are very good at talking without saying anything. Their empty speech is like the plain brown wrapper that people use to ship packages through the mail, so that their unassuming surfaces can conceal something insidious beneath.

Another important lesson has to do with the need for emotional honesty with oneself. So much of what I witnessed and experienced prior to tenure triggered in me a state of outrage, anger, sadness, and fear. Yet I was unwilling to admit these feelings openly, because it was just too difficult to acknowledge the facts of the matter versus being in emotional denial and sticking to the story that I told myself. In refusing to admit the truth and release these dark emotions, I carried them around in my gut until I became very, very sick. And I suffered until I was willing to come clean and be honest with myself and allow the appropriate expression of these feelings.

As this detachment became a practiced habit, not only did I learn how to live with a physically painful condition, but I went into a state of emotional numbness concerning my professional life. This went on, off and on, for the next three years until I received early tenure. The news was announced in May, and I had actually achieved something that I had dreamed about my entire life. You would think that I would be absolutely overjoyed. The problem was that, because of my practiced emotional detachment, I had gone numb and I couldn't feel anything. I realized that I had a problem when the people around me were so visibly happy and celebrating the news. Yet somehow, I couldn't be present to myself, and it felt like I was watching a movie play out on a screen in front of me rather than actually living my life.

Intuitively I knew that, because I was the one who had created this problem, I would have to be the one to resolve it, with the help of my Angelic Guides. Listening to their advice, I went into seclusion for an entire week, during which time I meditated for four to five hours a day and reflected deeply on my life. At the end of the week, I was exhausted but I also saw things with clarity. I saw the difference between the facts of the matter and the stories that I could no longer afford to tell myself, stories that often seemed to begin with the phrase, "No, that just can't be true…"

At the end of the week I sat on the couch eating my lunch. I began to relax and tears filled my eyes. Once the flow abated, I realized that I had been awarded tenure at an important research university, and I finally felt a surge of joy rising up in my being. As the tears cleared from my eyes, I looked up and saw my own Angelic Guides sitting on the couch beside me. They all had enormous smiles and they were wearing very festive, colorful party hats and carrying streamers, sparklers, and bouquets of flowers. One Angel put her arms around my shoulders, looked sweetly into my eyes, and said to the group, "Oh look, she's finally decided to show up at her own party." And then I started crying again.

### *Calling on the Angels to Practice Honesty and Let Go of Denial*

1. At the deepest level, you cannot lie to yourself or to the Angels. From time to time we all face extremely difficult situations. While rarely pleasant, these situations often provide tremendous opportunities for growth. Recognize this consciously and ask your Angelic Guides for their love and support.
2. Pay careful attention to the stories that you tell yourself, either about yourself or the people around you. Do the stories reflect the facts of the matter, or are they partial or convenient narratives that serve as coping mechanisms? Is there another voice competing for your attention? Do you have particular difficulty allowing yourself to

experience unpleasant emotions? If you feel or suspect that you are lying to yourself, seek help not only from the angelic realm but from a qualified professional.

3. Recall a time when you lied to yourself, or to someone else, about a situation that was too difficult to face. Was this something small and inconvenient, or did it concern a subject that felt nearly overwhelming? Remember how you compounded an already heavy burden through your resistance and untruthfulness. Do you recall ever being stuck by a lie and unable to shake its pattern? Did you even become physically ill from this situation? If so, what type of illness was it, and where did it manifest in your body? Then recall the circumstances when the truth became known, and how you felt afterward, physically, emotionally, and spiritually. Realize how much happier you were on the other side of the story. There is much wisdom in the saying that "the truth will set you free."
4. Do you regularly live in an unbalanced power dynamic? Do you live or work in a particularly competitive or adversarial environment? If so, you will need to pay careful attention to the wisdom of angelic and intuitive guidance. Respect the incoming information and proceed with caution regarding sharing information, expressing opinions, and articulating judgments aloud.
5. Pay careful attention to how people in power treat others, including those at their level, as well as those above and below them within a social hierarchy. Do not deny your empirical observations. Also observe whether a person's spoken language corresponds with the unspoken energy behind their words. Notice not only when people are lying, but pay attention to any gaps or discrepancies between what is said aloud and how the situation feels to you. Watch for patterns regarding the ways that words, energies, and behaviors correlate with one another.

6. Regularly practice shielding and protection. Imagine that you are completely surrounded by a shield of white light. While you can see everything clearly and interact with the world as you wish, no one can enter this protected space unless you allow them to.
7. If you have particularly difficult colleagues or family members, the Angels offer this exercise. In addition to the shielding described above, as you interact with these individuals and they begin talking to you, ask that their Angelic Guides (not your Guides, but theirs) place them in a glass telephone booth and close the door, so that they will be able to hear the sound of their own voices and feel the energies of their own words. After you have made this request, release everything completely and have no expectations regarding the outcome. Never wish the person any harm, just the capacity to hear and feel themselves speak.
8. As always, thank the Angels for their constant love, guidance, and protection.

# 28

# Enhancing Personal Power and Protection: The Warrior Weapon

This is another story which, unless you have actually experienced something like this, you may not believe it. But once again, this story is true. It teaches how you can protect and empower yourself once you realize that wounding instruments can be transformed into weapons of personal power. Once you recognize that weapons are embedded in your etheric body, you can reclaim them and transvalue the symbol. Through painful yet powerful experiences you can learn how to use the weapon as warriors do, through hit after hit after hit.

This story begins in childhood. Ever since I was very small, I have been highly sensitive and attuned to a broad spectrum of psychic and emotional energies. The shadow side of being clairsentient is that you feel everything intensely, and especially as a child, you may not understand much of what you are feeling, and it can be terrifying.

Sometimes the sadness of others would break my heart. And especially when I was young, being exposed to anger and fear would register discordantly in my body, and I would feel ill in the center of my body. The responses ranged from a mild case of butterflies in the stomach to full blown nausea and vomiting. As I grew up, I outgrew most of this pattern, although to this day I cannot tolerate violence or abusive behavior of any sort. As an adult, some of these old patterns resurfaced in the gastritis that I suffered before I received tenure. I would do very well for long stretches of time, and then some new issue would crop up that would invariably entail someone attempting to assert their power and dominance over others. These negative patterns are absolutely exhausting, and by the time I reached my early forties,

I had experienced more than enough unbalanced power dynamics to last a lifetime. While I could not change other people's attitudes or behaviors, I could certainly protect myself.

This story will sound incredibly cliché, but once again, this is how it actually happened. One evening I was down in the den working out on the elliptical machine. I was watching the original version of Sylvester Stallone's film *Rocky* which, as we all know, is about a talented underdog who stood up to the greatest challenge of his career, and who fought the powers that be and won. In my heart, I knew that this film was not only about boxing, but about the labors of Hercules and the warrior's grueling tests of strength that encompass the body, mind, heart, and especially, the spirit. As I was watching this film, I was watching a spiritual test, a knife that sliced through every part of the character's life as he rose to the occasion and won. The experiences of this teaching blade sharpened him greatly and changed his life.

Near the end of my workout, as I was watching the final sequence of the film, it felt as though I were watching a miniature movie of my own life play out in my mind's eye. Like a mini life review, I saw, felt, and sensed the energies not only of myself, but of other people as I witnessed all of the harsh trials that I had faced in order to earn—and win—the right to be myself, to have a voice and to walk in my own light. In that instant, I knew that I was more than equal to these challenges. With this recognition, I felt my spirit rise up in my body, and with my own eyes I saw that the reason why I had experienced such sensitivity in my gut was because *I had a very large sword embedded energetically in my midsection, a sword with an extremely powerful crystal blade and a sparkling silver handle*. (Can you *imagine* seeing such a thing etherically embedded in your body and in your being?) While still on the exercise machine, with my right hand I reached down into my own midsection and pulled the sword out by its silver handle and brandished it over my head.

This gesture of triumph felt absolutely amazing. The image that kept arising in my mind's eye was that of the young King Arthur pulling a sword out of a stone, except that in this case, both the sword and the stone were internal. Intuitively, I knew that my work was still not done. With my left hand, I reached into my stomach once again and pulled out a second sword that was a mirror reflection of the first but curved in the opposite direction. Then with both hands, I lifted the two swords over my head, forming an arch as the tips of the two crystal blades touched directly over the center of my head. I felt an incredible surge of power and, paradoxically, a tremendous sense of peace and well-being.

These long swords are made of crystalline light, and while they are two, they are one. The weapon is so large that I can actually get inside of it, and when I am standing inside, the crystal blade falls around me like a clear, protective shield. The long edges of the sword are razor sharp, and they can cut through stone. This sword is a beautiful and powerful shield of light. Like the teaching blades of Rocky's experiences, this sword comes from hundreds of difficult life lessons that taught me how to earn and recognize true power and its proper use.

Shortly after this happened, I faced yet another confrontation with an especially difficult colleague. I knew that I had to confront this person and address their behavior, and I also knew that I did not want to do this. I said to the Angelic Guides, "No matter what I say to this person, this situation is not going to be good." The Guides immediately replied, "No, this is you in your warrior position, and it is *not* a bad thing." I held these words and images closely in my mind and in my heart, and I said what needed to be said. Eventually, everything did resolve for the good of all involved.

Each and every one of us has unique gifts and abilities. One of the challenges that we all face concerns learning how to cultivate our gifts so that we are constantly growing and enriched. All the time, I ask the Angels to bring this into being, and it is such a joy to watch someone achieve something, and to see their light expand in the process. Unfortunately, I have also seen many situations where this is not the case. Instead of minding their business and focusing on themselves, people fall into patterns of competition and comparison, and the results are almost always anger, envy, greed, jealousy, and a dangerous tendency toward hierarchical judgments that entail seeing oneself and others as "superior" or "inferior." Undoubtedly, you have all seen this behavior, as well. In these difficult circumstances we must protect ourselves, for our own well-being and for the highest good of all involved. For these reasons, we all need our warrior weapons.

### *Building Your Warrior Weapon*

1. Remember that Light Workers are warriors, and that wounding instruments can be reclaimed and transformed into symbols of power. Ask yourself: In this lifetime, have I repeatedly been in situations where I have had to face hit after hit after hit? If so, what types of hits were they, and how did you respond? Did the hits seem to center on a particular location in the body? What types of patterns do you discern?
2. Practice conscious recognition, shielding, and protection, as described throughout this book.
3. If the blows tend to fall in a particular pattern, you will want to practice the healing exercise that the Archangel Raphael describes. In your mind, review a wounding experience, and watch as time slows down. Pay attention to the source and direction of the hit, and see if it crystallizes in a particular location. Then, view carefully the weapon (verbal, emotional, or physical) that the person used, and see if it needs to be lifted etherically out of your

body. If weapons are embedded in your etheric body, remove them and examine them carefully. Take the symbol and turn it around, so that you can use these items as a positive force to enhance personal power and protection. Note that blades are infinitely expandable, and that you can stretch a blade in your mind's eye so that it forms a protective shield all around you.

4. Reflect on the blows you have received and what the associated pain means to you. Was it as bad as you might have expected? Or was it better or worse? Realize that emotional hits may be more long-lasting and damaging than physical ones.
5. This story reflects the importance of an exercise program that maintains the strength of your intestinal muscles. These muscles are especially important when assuming poses of power and confidence.
6. Go to a martial arts school and watch some of the matches. Alternatively, go to a high school and observe how young athletes draw forth fortitude and courage before going into battle on the sports field. Watch how others do battle, and whether they show respect for their opponents.
7. Know that there are times when we all need to stand in our warrior positions, and that this is not a bad thing. Reflect on the ways in which you are stronger because of difficult situations you have faced. How have these experiences taught you valuable lessons about the proper use of power?

## 29

# Balancing Power and Delicacy: The Archangel Michael and St. Therese: He's the Cake, and She's the Frosting

This chapter contains another powerful yet tender story of angelic wisdom regarding issues of power, force, and the value of fighting for your own truth. The story teaches us how to temper the warrior spirit with sweetness and love in order to cultivate balance, self-love, and spiritual self-regard. An important part of my own spiritual development has come from working with my teacher, the medium Pat McKenna, and much of the information for this chapter was channeled through her.

In many ways, the story of my life is a story of great joys and great challenges. Again and again, the challenges have almost all had to do with finding myself in situations of unbalanced power that were not of my own creation, but which I had to negotiate carefully. Thus many times in my life I have found it necessary to be walking as a warrior with a shield in front of me and two swords at each side. What else could I do? When I'm in this warrior stance, I am able to connect with the golden light of clarity and the purple color of healing. The gold and the purple conduct the high omnipresence of clarity of intuition, divine love, and spirit presence. These are the colors of the Archangel Michael, who is a force of tremendous power. When Michael appears, there is always so much purple and gold. He often stands behind me, literally protecting my back, drawing my shoulders down and lifting my head up higher. His light and his power are so intense that, when he draws near, I feel a flush of warmth, like a flame running through me, and I find it very difficult not to start crying because his love and his power are so beautiful. Michael is both the sword and the shield. He is a force beyond force and a light beyond light and a love beyond love.

When discussing the difficulties I have encountered in my life, Michael tells me, "Never forget that you are a staunch soul. You have worked so hard and so diligently in so many situations that, if I stated them all for you, you would become ill. And now, I don't want you to start throwing up." (Yes, he actually said exactly these words to me.) A part of me started laughing wryly at my response to such perpetual difficulties: "Great, just great. Another lifetime, another day at the office." Yet just as there is levity, there is also gravity and great seriousness of purpose. Michael tells me that in many lifetimes, "People have wanted to put you in the closet and feel bad about yourself." Through Pat, Michael tells me that a part of me is sad that I've always had to fight for my own truth: "You can't stand power over other beings, and the endless stories of defeat." Yet he says that it's "just a play, a drama that people endlessly play out. Acknowledge the dance. The players want acknowledgement, so acknowledge the drama and move on. Now, your mission is changing. Part of your mission is an acceptance of being the warrior in any and all circumstances. The movement is already in place. There is no need for you to be in harm's way again." That is the cake.

Thus for all the difficulties I have faced, I have also been gifted with tremendous love and angelic assistance. One form of this gift appears like a cloud of amorphous white light, which resembles the Milky Way. In conjunction with this white light, the Guides tell me that running water also cleanses. It generates white light, and both the water and the light are conducive to auric cleansing. In part, when we sit quietly and watch running water, this act can turn the mind inward so that there can be cleansing internally.

At the spiritual level, there is also a lot of pink adornment on me. My etheric body wears something that resembles a shawl. It is solid pink and very beautiful. If you were to stare into it, it would look like pure silk that is a very pale white-gold, yet the shawl is pure pink. This is my mantle, and it protects the heart center. The mantle exacerbates love, self-love, dignity, and courage. Both the amorphous white light and the pink mantle are gifts from the Archangel Michael and from St. Therese. I have always had a close relationship with St. Therese, who is known as the Little Flower. St. Therese is not only a brilliant thinker, but she is a sweet spirit and a gentle presence who is as humble as she is beautiful. Her work is always about dedication to the goodness of love.

Sometimes I see little bouquets of etheric flowers floating around me. These bouquets are gifts from St. Therese. Some of these exquisite miniature bouquets are composed of purple and white violets, while others are of miniature pink spray roses, and still others are of white lilies and chrysanthemums. The flowers resemble diminutive bundles of light tied with bright, colorful ribbons. The Little Flower carries such miniature bouquets that light up everything around them. The bouquets are gifts to inspire safety, confidence, and illumination. The bouquets also express a mystical paradox. Because they are so delicate, they are so powerful. Because they are so small, they are so big.

My middle name is Therese, and I am actually named for this particular saint. My first name, Marcia, is the feminine form of Marcus, which means "Dedicated to Mars," the god of war. Thus the name Marcia signifies someone who is proud and martial; it is the name of a warrior. Taken together, the Archangel Michael and St. Therese form an incredible team of power and delicacy, of masculine and feminine energies. Michael goes anywhere. He moves and removes obstacles. He does the battle, while St. Therese brings in the sweetness. He's the cake, and she's the frosting.

The Angels tell me that, what they wish for me and for all of us here on this planet is that our sense of "Divine love and compassionate love are equal in the ones to whom we're speaking as it is for us." They tell me that this sense of equality between the human and angelic realms is the touch of divine love and of self-love. That is the cake, and that is the frosting.

### *Experiencing Power and Delicacy with the Archangel Michael and St. Therese*

1. Michael is the most powerful Archangel and a master of the proper use of force. St. Therese is a source of incredible sweetness and gentleness. Call upon the Archangel Michael and St. Therese when you need to balance great power with great delicacy.
2. Ask the Archangel Michael for help whenever you need power and protection, particularly when walking through threatening environments, negotiating unbalanced power dynamics, or having to be strong and brave to fight for your own truth and stand up for yourself or others. Unfortunately, there are those who seek to make themselves powerful by taking power from others. Be consciously attuned to such individuals and call on the Archangel Michael for guidance and support.
3. As Michael says, if you find yourself constantly confronting unequal power dynamics, acknowledge that this is just a play, a kind of perpetual human drama. Acknowledge the players and move on.
4. To maintain an open heart, call on St. Therese to protect your heart center. See her as a cherished source of sweetness and love, and thank her for being present in your life.
5. Notice how things that are small and delicate can also be quite large and powerful. Feel the joy of this spiritual paradox.

# IV

# How to Connect with the Mystical Dimensions of the Natural World

# 30

# Joining the Archangel Ariel's Retinue: White Tipped Wings: Lifting the Light

The Angels can help you to become more sensitive to the natural world and its innate divinity. Working with your conscious mind and your intuitive guidance, the Angels can encourage you to engage in actions that promote environmental awareness. When you participate in such activities, you provide much-needed assistance to the planet and to other beings.

This story is very close to my heart. In my ideal morning routine, I wake up gently to National Public Radio (NPR), and I lie in bed for about twenty minutes listening to world events. Then, my husband comes upstairs carrying a hot drink and a small bag of food so that I can hand feed and brush my beautiful cat, Luna. She walks over and says good morning as soon as my husband goes downstairs. Then the cat and I listen to the radio together, and we both start our day very softly and gently. As we sit together on the bed, I will often see small flashing sparkles of extremely bright, silvery-white light as the Angels join us for these lovely moments together. And sometimes when I am holding Luna close, with her head tucked under my chin, I will see a very bright white light appear behind my closed eyes. Just as it sounds, this is all very peaceful and intimate, and I'm very happy to say that I begin nearly every day with this scenario.

But one morning I woke up half an hour early, which rarely happens. Something just didn't feel right. It wasn't that I was in pain or felt sick, but I was definitely feeling uneasy. One part of me thought, "This is interesting, because it's so unusual. I wonder what's going on..." Another part of me told the first part to be quiet and responded, "Oh crap. I wonder what mess I'm going to have to clean up now..." As I was lying in bed having this internal debate, the alarm clock radio and the buzzer went off simultaneously. This has never happened before, as the clock is always set to the radio, so I knew that something was going on. I was already half awake, but this very odd sound woke me up abruptly. I sat up and checked and, sure enough, the little clock was set only to the radio, and so I started thinking, "What next?"

I didn't have long to wait. A few minutes later my husband walked into the bedroom. Except that, instead of carrying the usual hot drink, his hands were empty and he was wearing a pair of blue latex gloves. Seeing this, I immediately assumed that the plumbing was leaking somewhere and I prayed that the problem wouldn't be too severe. It turned out that it wasn't the plumbing.

Instead, I heard him say, "Good Morning. We have a problem."

"What is it, Sweetie?"

"We have a dove with a broken wing. It was lying on the back patio. I've put it into a Sherpa Bag, which I put in the closet so that the cats wouldn't disturb it."

I got up and looked in the closet. Sure enough, there was the dove. With great care, I gently looked into the Sherpa Bag. The bird seemed to be in good shape overall, other than its wing. After some brief conversation, we decided that we would go together to the Wildlife Center of Texas. There, the bird would receive care, the wing would be X-rayed and splinted, and after rehabilitation, the bird would be released. This is just what we did, and an hour and a half later I was back in the house recording all of this in my journal.

I know that this event happened for several reasons. One reason was so that my husband could be introduced to this wildlife rehabilitation center, so that he could see it physically and know where it was and the type of work that goes on there. Another reason was so that I could put this story into *The Angels In Between*. The Angelic Guides ask that we all say a little prayer, in our minds and hearts, for the assistance and well-being of all injured birds and wildlife. Amen.

Ariel, the Archangel of Nature, tells me that she always hears us when we call to her for help with an injured animal. She tells me that we are not alone in caring for nature and for the planet: "We have a retinue of beings on the planet who are doing this work, but they don't necessarily know it." The Angels tell me that "Divine presence is in all things. It is in me, it is in you, it is in everyone, and it is in every particle, in every bit of bark and leaf on every tree. All are part of the goodness of divine love." Often when I walk, I pick up trash as I go along. Not paper, but non-biodegradable materials such as plastic, glass, metal, and Styrofoam. While this behavior may look a little eccentric, this is the least of my concerns. The results are completely worthwhile because I know that our environment is cleaner and greener as a result.

Many of you reading this book may well be part of this group, working to assist the natural world. If so, please know that you are not alone. You are part of Ariel's retinue, and we are all working together to lift the light.

In lifting the light, you as a human being are using your wings. Those wings are as tender and beautiful as the white-tipped wings of the dove.

Because my husband was instrumental in providing this lovely, vulnerable being with immediate care and assistance, he acted as the bird's Angel. In my heart, I know that dove will be with him, always.

## *Working with Nature Angels*

1. Recognize that the natural world *is* the divine world, and that human beings are part of the natural world, and thus we are all part of the divinity of nature.
2. The next time you hold a beloved pet, see if bright lights shine behind your closed eyes. Open your eyes and see if

you can discern little sparkling lights or shifting energies around your pet.

3. Make time to visit animals in shelters or pet stores who are isolated and lonely. Support "no kill shelters"—where volunteers foster an animal until it finds a permanent home—with cash, food, or toys. Consider adopting one of these souls in transition, and encourage others to do so, as well.
4. Older pets, like older people, have special needs and may not receive the attention they once did when they were younger and more energetic. Engage these creatures to bring them joy and remind them of their special place in the world.
5. Become familiar with the location and services of wildlife shelters near your home. Develop a plan so that you can respond quickly if and when you come across an injured bird or animal. If you feel drawn to the shelter, consider volunteering there or supporting their work philanthropically.
6. Say this little prayer, in your mind and in your heart:

*Dearest Angels,*
*Please assist, and promote the wellbeing, of all animals, birds, and wildlife, particularly those that are hurt or injured.*
*Amen*

7. When you walk outside, consider picking up trash as you go along. Paper is less important than non-degradable materials such as glass, metal, plastics, and Styrofoam. Encourage others to do this, as well.
8. If you work in an office, recycle as much paper as possible. Use both sides of the sheet in your printing.
9. Perform all actions gently with a loving heart, and give thanks for the beauty of the natural world.

# 31

# Melting the Distinctions Between the Sacred and the Profane: "We Look Like the Sky": What Blue Means to a Blue Jay

As you consciously recognize the divinity of the natural world, you begin to approach the world in a new way. The mystical sense of being in multiple places at once can help you to collapse artificial distinctions and man-made categories. Such expanded thinking represents a powerful form of the arts of allowance and self-overcoming. Living this way will help you forge new and unexpected connections between different realms of being. One of the most powerful and surprising examples of these blended categories concerns the relations between the sacred and the profane.

Although we live in a fairly urban area of Houston, we are fortunate to have majestic live oak trees in front of the house, and a large old elm tree in the backyard. These trees are the homes of many birds—including doves, pigeons, cardinals, sparrows, pileated woodpeckers, robins, wrens, goldfinches, hummingbirds, and blue jays. Some birds are migratory, while others are permanent residents. By the elm tree in the backyard, we put out seed blocks and we place loose seed in a wooden tray, and our modest yard seems to be a miniature bird paradise. Every time I look at these ordinary sights, I am struck by how extraordinary they are. The familiar world of trees and birds is filled with complexity, perfection, and beauty. Every day I try to devote some conscious recognition to the idea that multiple worlds are brought together within me when I express love and gratitude to the natural world. As we lift "ordinary" life up to the heavens, we bring the heaven world down to the earth. Our conscious recognition of these twinned processes becomes like an infinity sign, a hinge point where the visible becomes visionary, and vice versa. The Angelic Guides tell me that bringing conscious recognition into a situation is a way to channel intensity, much the way that a beam of sunlight can be directed through a magnifying glass to intensify light. The Angels say that channeling such a beam of light is a way to enhance spiritual presence, much like the intensity of the words burning up the pages of this book when you read the sentences and have an instant hit of recognition.

As lofty and sacred as all of this sounds, it is also charmingly simple. In part, it's a matter of consciously recognizing sights and patterns that have become so ingrained and familiar as to be automatic and nearly invisible. Recognition is like breathing new life into a mode of living and making it conscious again. As you express love and gratitude for the beauty of the world around you—if you aren't doing this already—you will be able to see the sacred in every part of the tree, in every aspect of the bird. This is especially wonderful because the trees and the birds have always stood as such familiar presences, and they are standing before your eyes right now.

On the subject of bringing worlds together, of lifting the earth to the heavens and bringing spirit presence down to the earth, let me tell you what a blue jay once said to me. One afternoon, as I was reflecting on how grateful I was for the trees and the birds and all of the worlds that were simultaneously present in my own backyard and in myself, I focused on the blue jays, and I came into a state of telepathic communication with them. I asked them to tell me a bit about themselves, and after emphasizing how much they adored peanuts, they said, "*We too are multiple. We are many things at once. We look like the sky, and when we fly, we bring the blue heavens down to the green earth. We bring life to life. This is what blue means to a blue jay.*"

### *Recognizing the Sacredness of the Natural World*

1. Practice overcoming the distinctions between the sacred and the profane. Look out your window and notice what you see. When you see a familiar sight, such as a pet who shares your home, or the birds that live in your trees, recognize that these beings are both sacred and profane, spiritual and worldly, just as you are. Know that everything exists in multiple states simultaneously. As you practice this knowledge, you are thinking like a mystic.
2. Understand the seasons and what they mean, not only to animals, but to the trees and plants, and to you.
3. Exercise care when cleaning up your yard, such as raking up piles of leaves where toads or other creatures may have built their homes. If possible, dedicate a portion of your yard to nature and do not cultivate it. Consider meditating outside in this natural environment.
4. Observe how the animals enjoy the environment you create or the food you leave for them, and how they show gratitude.
5. Express love and gratitude to the natural world on a regular basis. When you consciously recognize the divinity of the natural world, you reach a place where your own vision becomes a form of prayer.

## 32

# Recognizing the Divinity of the Natural World: The Light Bodies of Birds

Every living being has a soul, and sometimes we are privileged to be allowed to see it. If you keep this in mind as you walk through your daily life, this thought will enhance your understanding of the intrinsic divinity of the world that we all inhabit, humans and nonhumans alike.

As I walk through my own life, I will often discover incredibly beautiful things that sometimes appear in unexpected places. When this happens, my skin tingles, especially in my hands, and I get goose-flesh on my arms. Sometimes I will even point this out to other people, so that they too can see that something beautiful is happening right now. At that moment, the magic is in our midst and all around us.

This thrill of recognition often comes when I engage with nature. Sometimes when I focus on the incredible beauty of the doves and pigeons in my backyard, I will look deeply into their black and golden eyes, and a world of peace will open up. The eyes of birds can be gateways to paradise. Something beautiful and nearly impossible is happening in those fragile moments, and its wings just brushed against the corners of our world.

Beyond my own backyard, the Tropical Bird House at the Houston Zoo is one of my favorite places. In this open-air aviary, many varieties of tropical birds fly freely in a lush garden setting filled with green plants and flowing water. A glass skylight allows for natural illumination, while visitors pass over the wooden walkway and stone bridge that run through the center of the aviary. The Tropical Bird House is a sacred space. As soon as you enter this alternative, miniature world, there is a palpable shift of atmosphere and energy, of light and flight, as you are privileged to visit the home of a special community of birds.

Because the Tropical Bird House is such an extraordinary place, during a visit there I asked the heaven world for a message about birds that I could include in this book. Having made this request, I stood in a quiet corner and watched the birds flying all around me. After a few minutes, a very beautiful bird perched on a nearby branch. I later learned that the bird is a golden-breasted starling, or royal starling. This bird's breast and lower body are bright golden yellow, his throat an iridescent violet purple, and his wings are pure black. As you can imagine, this bird is absolutely beautiful. Initially, he perched on a branch a few feet away from where my husband and I were standing. Gradually he hopped closer to us, and he paused for several minutes on the stone railing about a foot away from where we stood. As he came closer, I felt my heart expanding with joy, and I expressed gratitude to everyone who could hear my silent voice.

As this gorgeous bird perched on the stone railing, his body shifted before my eyes. The bird showed me that he was made not only of the feathers and beak and claws that people could observe with their physical eyes, but that he was also made of golden light. I was reminded of the relationship between human bodies and their auras that I was shown so long ago at the Post Office. This bird showed me an amorphous field of golden light that was very large, perhaps three to four times the size of his body, and it constantly shifted softly around his physical form. It appeared as if this etheric field of glowing golden light not only surrounded the bird, but that the bird lived inside this luminous field, much the way that chicks inhabit a nest.

I thanked the bird for the gift of this encounter, and the bird asked me to convey the message that *all* birds and wildlife consist not only of their physical bodies, but of such subtle luminous fields. The bird emphasized that this is an important message for readers of this book, namely that what most people see with their eyes is just the merest fraction of animals' total existence and their absolute glory. Before he flew off to join his mate, this beautiful bird thanked me for weaving his gold into this text.

### *Seeing the Auras of Birds*

1. Know that not only human beings, but all living beings have an aura, or halo of light, that surrounds and accompanies their physical bodies. Also know that there is much more to animals' existence than meets the eye. The next time you are outside observing wild animals, say a prayer of gratitude and ask that you be allowed to perceive an animal's aura.
2. The steps for seeing an animal's aura are much the same as for discerning a human aura. Review the process outlined at the beginning of this book. Bear in mind that an animal's aura may not necessarily be brightest around its head, and that the light may be most intense around the center of its body. The light field may be several times the size of an animal's physical form and constantly shifting.
3. Listen carefully to the sounds that animals make and discern their songs and vocalizations. Observe how animals communicate both verbally and nonverbally. Pay special attention to how an animal interacts with its mate.
4. Regularly visit a zoo, park, or aquarium, and build your relationships with a few species of animals that you visit over time. Be selective and pay attention to animals that you feel particularly drawn to. Do not rush through to try to see as many animals as possible.
5. These exercises take a lot of practice, so do not become discouraged. As with seeing auras, keep practicing until you are able to see animals' light bodies.

# 33

# Appreciating the Harmony Between the Parts and the Whole: The Palm Elemental and the Heart of the Hand

Studying the relationships between the parts and the whole of plant life can give you a heightened appreciation of the relationship between inner and outer harmony. I first learned this valuable lesson when I was an undergraduate at Mount Holyoke College. I would spend hours visiting the Talcott Greenhouse, a series of late-nineteenth-century glasshouses with a tropical conservatory. Not only did this luminous living environment inspire a deep sense of inner calm, peace, and wonder, but the plants helped me to recognize the many ways in which our outer physical world includes profound metaphorical and metaphysical dimensions. While plants embody this multiplicity in a marvelous variety of ways, the palm offers a striking example for you to consider.

I love to read before falling asleep at night. Short stories, poetry, novels, mysteries, and spiritual writings are my favorites. I hope that many of you are reading *The Angels In Between* before you fall asleep and enter the dreamtime.

Late at night I often read in my home office, which is a corner room with two sets of double windows facing south and east. The south windows look out onto the back garden, while the east windows are perched in the canopy of an elm tree. As I stretch out reading on the chaise in my office, I have a view of the nighttime sky through both sets of windows.

One night, after I finished reading and turned out the light, I lay quietly thinking about how much I loved the lush green landscape of Houston. In our own yard, we are fortunate to have several lovely old trees, including live oaks in the front yard, and a large old elm tree in the back. Among the many ground plantings are different varieties of palms. Ever since childhood I have loved the leafy green fronds of palms. However, palm trees are not native to the cold climate of New England. Yet because we only rarely get a hard frost in Houston, we're able to have a variety of exotic subtropical plants, including two different types of palms.

As I lay on the chaise, I contemplated my special fondness for palms. As I reflected on these plants, the Palm Elemental paid me a visit with a special message for this book. The Palm Elemental is a beautiful luminous green color, and he gave a male appearance. Resembling the plant itself, he is very tall and lean, like a plant stalk, and his head is crowned with individual palm fronds. His message concerns harmonious interactions between the parts and the whole.

He showed me that the palm teaches the lesson of harmonious configurations of forms, and he emphasized the similarities between the plant and the human worlds. In both cases, the Palm Elemental asks us to observe how individual units work together to form cohesive patterns. The pattern is greater than the sum of its parts. When people come together to form communities—groups that can include families, classes, offices, organizations, and so forth—a living pattern forms that is made up of living individuals. Like the people of which it is composed, the pattern has its own organic life form; in fact, it *is* a life form, a form that is alive and constantly evolving, growing and changing.

Human beings also have a palm at the center of their hands, and the Palm Elemental tells me that the palm is the heart of the hand. The palm is the central point around which the individual units of the fingers branch off to form numerous shapes, gestures, and configurations as they perform different tasks and communicate in a variety of expressive ways.

In all cases, whether the forms are those of the plant kingdom, groups of human beings, or the elements of the human hand, palms represent the harmonious interactions between the parts and the whole, between the center and the edges, and between individuals and the larger patterns that they form, which are themselves ever-changing configurations of life.

### *Recognizing the Harmony Between the Parts and the Whole*

1. Study a tree leaf, not as a familiar and insignificant object, but as a miniature version of a complex organizational structure. Observe the shape and design of the leaf, as well as its details and patterns of organization. Notice how one section leads to the next and how the parts relate to the whole. Study the tree that the leaf originally came from, and observe how hundreds of such leaves play a role in creating the life of the plant. Allow yourself to feel wonder and admiration for nature's complexity.
2. How do you feel when you are interacting closely with plants? Do you feel better after spending time in nature?
3. Find plantings in your yard that are overgrown and can be split and replanted. Broken pieces of plants can also easily be found in parks and outside restaurants.
4. Start plants from seeds and enjoy watching them grow. Don't be despondent if they do not survive; instead, learn from this.
5. Some plants, such as lilies and poinsettia, are given during the holidays and expected to be thrown away afterward. "Save" a few of these plants and make them part of your world.
6. Find a palm leaf and repeat the exercise outlined in step 1. If you do not have access to an actual palm leaf, find a picture of one on the Internet.
7. Look closely at the palm of your own hand and repeat the exercise again. Pay special attention to the ways that the

parts relate to the whole, and how your own hands form a constantly shifting pattern. Again, consciously allow yourself to recognize the complexity and the harmony of all that you are viewing, and pay attention to how this knowledge makes you feel.

8. As you contemplate the relations between the parts and the whole, reflect on any social groups that you are part of. They can include families as well as professional organizations. View the structure of the group abstractly. What is its overall shape and pattern? Are its edges smooth and rounded or jagged and sharp? When everything is working well and flowing harmoniously, what are the relationships between the parts and the whole? And, when things are not working harmoniously, how does the structure appear? Does one part become much larger and dominate the others, causing the form to become unbalanced? If the form is out of balance, can the parts relate to one another effectively, or does movement become awkward or even frozen? What is your position in this structure? Are you at its center or at its edges? How does your presence contribute to the whole? How is the whole greater than the sum of the parts? How does the group form a living pattern? Can you sense the energy and the life of this structure?

# 34

# Living in an Illuminated Landscape: The Light on the Water

The extraordinary resides within the ordinary, and miraculous things can be seen in everyday life. As you cultivate a heightened sense of mystical consciousness, you may have unusual experiences in nature, especially as you recognize that the land and the water are full of living spiritual presences. As always, ask your Angelic Guides to help you experience this illuminated landscape.

Several years ago, on a bright Sunday afternoon in November, my husband and I took a trip to Galveston. Galveston is a coastal Texas city located on Galveston Island, with sandy beaches surrounding water that leads to Galveston Bay on one side, and to the Gulf of Mexico on the other. The beaches of Galveston are very different from those surrounding the Atlantic and Pacific Oceans. While those salty ocean waters are very dark blue and often feature rocky stretches with high waves and foaming white crests, the waters surrounding Galveston are silver-brown, and the waves are much gentler. Sitting on the beach in Galveston, you see stretches of light brown sand, silver-brown sea, and endless points of sunlight shining on the water.

Galveston Island State Park has a wonderful beach on the seashore, and that's where we sat on that gorgeous autumn afternoon. It was still warm, but the summer heat had largely receded. My husband and I walked up and down the beach, and then we sat quietly on some wooden benches. I reflected on how I was always so busy, as I was not only teaching full-time and performing numerous administrative and service tasks, but I was doing the research and writing on one of my scholarly monographs. However, that particular Sunday afternoon I was tired, and so I decided that I was going to take a few hours off from the work that always seemed to engulf me on all sides, like the waters that surrounded the tiny island. Given that I was around so much natural beauty, I decided that I would enjoy a state of contemplation and reflective gratitude.

I sat very quietly on the wooden bench with my feet plunged into the warm, shifting sand. When we sit like this at the beach, our bodies actually sink a little way into the earth, and physically and spiritually, we merge with the planet. Gazing at the waves rippling along the open water, I expressed my love and gratitude for this world and its endless natural beauty. As I said this prayer, it felt as though I were sinking down and rising up at once. Everything became very quiet, and it felt like time slowed down, and then time stopped entirely. I felt like I was merging and rising, again and again.

And then I saw the lights on the water. They appeared just below the horizon line, in the open expanse where the sky meets the water. In that zone, the atmosphere started to shimmer and glow. Everything around me became very white, and the whiteness was filled with small, delicate black outlines of what appeared to be cellular membranes. If it hadn't been a warm November afternoon in Texas, I could almost have imagined that I was watching a snowstorm in Boston. Almost, but not quite. The beings that I saw did not resemble snowflakes. Their bodies were more elongated and cellular than crystalline, and they looked like falling raindrops.

Amazingly, there were tens of thousands of individual shimmering beings who floated in the field of white light that had arisen between the air and the water. Above all, I was struck not only by their beauty, but by the enormity of the multitude. They were water spirits and their bodies were etheric, having form but not substance. While they clearly had individual forms, I couldn't discern any facial features. They were constantly moving and shimmering, as if hovering in a mist that was also a kind of dance, a dance that floated on the breath of their collective movements. Instinctively, I knew that these beings kept this landscape alive as they rose up off the water. They were cleansing and purifying presences, lightening and enlivening the landscape.

I could both see and feel their delicate, magical presences as our worlds touched. Even as I remained in my physical body, sitting on the wooden bench with my feet in the sand, I was also a part of this immersive, shimmering world that had come to life all around me. As they surrounded my husband and me in their swirl of movement, the earth felt lighter and less solid, more magical and etheric. I became one with the light on the water.

It's hard to say exactly how long this experience lasted. Once again, time slowed down and the landscape assumed a hyper-clarity and intense sharpness of focus. When this occurs I always have a sense of being suspended between worlds, of being in multiple places at once. After sitting with these beings for a while, I expressed my profound joy and gratitude for the gift of this encounter. Then, I watched with my physical eyes as the misty field of etheric beings gradually dissolved and cleared before me. Slowly, the world returned to normal, but this is the "new normal" of knowing that our everyday world is filled with the presence of living light, etheric magic, and shimmering grace.

### *Sensing the Mystical Dimensions of the Natural World*

1. As with all of the exercises in this book, recognize that there is much more to the world than we can ever see or know with our human senses. Allow yourself to feel awe and wonder at the grandeur of the natural world, and give thanks for being part of it all.
2. Sit quietly in a natural location and know that this space is filled with living presences, including those that are visible and those that are not. Connect deeply with this

location and sense its unique energy. How does it feel to be in this space, and what is distinctive about it? Ask your Angelic Guides to open your heart and your eyes to the living world all around you.

3. Sit in a state of quiet contemplation and reflective gratitude. In this heightened spiritual state, see if the appearance of the world shifts before your eyes. Do you notice details that you wouldn't ordinarily see? Can you discern light forms moving around plants or animals? Pay careful attention to how you feel when engaging so deeply with the landscape.
4. Visit a place with a secluded fountain or pool of water. Breathe deeply and relax. Take note of anything that arises in your field of view. Make this a regular routine to help cleanse your spirit.
5. Periodically visit national, state, or local parks during quiet times and off-seasons. Take time to be alone with nature. Gather a few leaves, needles, rocks, or shells to contemplate at home. The sights and scents of these items can bring back memories of the trip. Work on making part of your home more of a natural environment and meditate there.
6. Express love and gratitude to your Angelic Guides and to the natural world, and record your experiences in a journal.

# 35

# Returning to the Mountain

Within the natural world, there are locations that hold extraordinary amounts of spiritual power. I have experienced such power by the ocean, within national parks, and especially, by the mountains. In the first part of this book, I describe the powerful mystical awakening that I experienced at the Superstition Mountain in Arizona. Several years later my husband and I returned to the Phoenix area for a brief vacation, and on Christmas day, I was guided to visit the mountain again.

As we approached the mountain, I noticed that the car was filled with Angels. They started tickling my ears and playing with my hair and earrings. They greeted me with laughter and told me that I was being recalled because the mountain wanted me home. As we drew closer to the mountain, my psychic senses became heightened, and I distinctly heard one spirit say to another, "This is our Daughter who works with those who are passing into the light and struggling against the darkness. She's approaching now." My Angelic Guides told me that I was being honored because of my work, and I started crying softly.

For about an hour I sat at the base of the mountain, reconnecting with the sacredness of the site. With my physical eyes I saw that I was surrounded by a shower of silver white sparks, and that a great deal of light and energy were shifting all around me. Then hundreds of Angels appeared as balls of white light. Looking up, I noticed that the top of the mountain was also haloed in this white light. As I reflected on the beauty of all that I was seeing, the messages started coming through. I was told, "As you sit and meditate, you are seeing the power of the mountain behind your closed eyes." The Angels then said that, from that point onward, the mountain was within me, behind my eyes and within my life, giving me strength and power. They told me that I'll no longer be doing things simply because certain things are expected of me, or because the "system" I live in expects me to be living a certain way. Now I'll be living for myself and doing what I know in my heart is right. The Angelic Guides summed it up as they told me, "When you give yourself the power, you give us the power."

Sitting quietly at the base of the mountain, hearing those words on Christmas day, the white light was so brilliant, and it was coming into my eyes so quickly, that I was living a sacred paradox. I was seeing so much that I almost couldn't see.

## *Visiting Places of Power*

1. Natural landscapes—such as mountains, oceans, forests, caves, and Native sacred sites—can be places of extraordinary power. Visit one of these locations during a quiet time. If possible, seek out lesser known spaces in more remote locations. Chat with the park rangers or guides and ask if there is anything special you should look for seasonally, such as a natural waterfall, beaver dams, nests of bird hatchings, etc.
2. Find a place where you can sit quietly and not be disturbed by others. Ask your Angelic Guides to accompany you throughout this visit, to offer protection and guidance, and to heighten your awareness. Express your gratitude for their presences and for this unique landscape.
3. In a state of quiet contemplation, go without and go within. First, carefully observe the distinctive features of the landscape and its physical appearance. Then close your eyes and meditate at this site. Follow the meditation steps outlined at the beginning of this book. Open your mind and allow yourself to connect with this space. Be

receptive to any messages or images that arise in your mind's eye. Is there a particular image or symbol that keeps appearing? If so, pay careful attention because you will want to work with this power symbol after your visit, as you reengage your familiar life. Then, open your eyes and look carefully at the landscape again. Is it the same landscape as before, or has its appearance shifted in a subtle way? Consciously recognize the changes, both in the appearance of the outer world and within yourself, and notice how you feel. Do you feel calm and peaceful, or energized and empowered? Above all, look up at the sky and see if you can discern energetic presences moving in the sky above you. Allow yourself ample time to transition gently between states of consciousness.

4. As always, express gratitude for the gift of this place, and record your experiences in a journal.

# V

# How to Recognize the Mystical Dimensions of the End of Life and How to Help People Leave with Grace

# 36

# Receiving a Message from the Afterlife: "I'm Calling to Invite You to a Party in Heaven"

Just as the Angel of Inner Peace and Harmony teaches the great lesson of the reconciliation of opposites, brining diverse elements together in a state of unity, I have also experienced worlds converging in the relationship between life and the afterlife. This true story shows how life can continue after life, and it asks you to consider that humanity *is* part of the heaven world, just as the heaven world resides within the human domain.

Undoubtedly like many of you, I have lost several dear friends to cancer. Because I have worked in a cancer center for a number of years, this does not make the situation any easier when this disease touches the life of someone close to me. While this illness can be heartbreaking, I have also seen first-hand the ways that it can produce pure spiritual gold. It's as if the person is undergoing the trials of fire, and they are put in a furnace of alchemical transformation from which they often emerge with extreme insight, wisdom, and love.

One spring afternoon a very close friend of mine received a terrible diagnosis: she had advanced pancreatic cancer, with a large inoperable tumor and evidence of aggressive metastasis. Being a professor, her first step was to seek information. She researched the most comprehensive cancer treatments available, and she entered one of the nation's leading cancer centers to undergo a regimen of combined therapies. Intellectually, she knew that the odds of a five year survival horizon were well below ten percent, but she always fought hard, saying that she could be part of that group. Given all that I have witnessed, I can only say that individual cases are always complex and each situation is unique. Despite the most powerful combination therapies available, my friend's condition progressively deteriorated. She became increasingly frail and experienced pain on so many levels. Her last days were spent quietly in hospice care, where she passed away. Because this woman cherished life so deeply and had fought so hard against her illness, her untimely death brought great sadness to many people whose lives she had touched. Her passing touched my own life in a special and wonderful way.

My friend had been quite interested in spiritual subjects, and early on she was one of the very few people in academia who knew about my "double life" as a clairvoyant. I will always be so grateful to her for her respect and generosity; I will always love her for that. Because she knew about this part of my life, she came to me in spirit after her passing. At the end of the day, people cannot help but be who they are. Characteristically, my friend came to me in a very playful and even slightly mischievous way to give me a message.

It was the afternoon of the day she passed. Physically, I was thousands of miles away where, as usual, I was sitting at my desk, working absorbedly at my computer. Deeply engaged in the book I was writing, I heard the phone at my side ring softly. It was a very unusual ring, short and quick, and the bell was fainter than normal. I picked up the receiver, but no one was there, so I put it back in its cradle and turned back to my own text. A moment later it happened again. I heard a very brief faint ring, and no one was on the other end. For a moment I experienced a flash of annoyance, and I seriously hoped that there wasn't a short in the line, and that this would be yet another problem with a household appliance, and where was I going to find the time to have the damned thing repaired, and so forth.

This flash of annoyance was followed by my hearing soft but hearty peals of laughter. And then I had a blazing flare of insight, and I recognized what was happening. Without being told or receiving any external news, I knew that my friend had just passed and that she was now in the heaven world. And I knew that there was a *major* celebration going on. This woman knew how to celebrate life, and there was one heck of a party on the other side. I had vivid, flashing glimpses of curly silver and golden streamers flying through the air, champagne corks popping in every direction, and my friend's distinctive laughter ringing at the center of the celebration. And then I knew that she was using the phone to give me the message, not only that she had passed on and made her journey safely, but she was calling to invite me to a party in heaven! In joy and recognition, I cried softly and I started celebrating with her.

Several hours later that evening, it happened again. I was passing by a different telephone, and the phone gave the same very short, faint ring as I walked by. This time I didn't bother to pick up the receiver. I didn't need to. I got the message. I thanked my friend and told her how happy I was for her, and how much I loved her. And of course, I thanked her for inviting me to her party in heaven, which was nothing but light and joy. The phone has never rung like that again.

### *Interacting with People at the End of Life and Recognizing Those Who Have Recently Crossed Over*

1. When people receive news of a devastating illness, or when they become extremely physically sick, often the logical portion of their mind will close down and the emotional pathway will become ignited. Be prepared for this. Particularly when people are feeling vulnerable, they will appreciate a connection to your strength, groundedness, and emotional support. Practice compassion as fully as possible.
2. Observe the ways in which approaching the end of life can dramatically shape a person's perspective. Be aware

of such shifts, both in the person and in yourself as you interact with them.

3. As is the case with each person's life, each person's death is unique. Listen to the advice of professional caregivers, but also know that every person is a complex individual being.
4. Understand that life and death are natural processes, and that both are part of a single continuum of being. In many ways, life and the afterlife are two aspects of a single state of the soul. Be aware of the ways in which the end of life represents an opportunity for extraordinary occurrences and for the convergence of different states of being. Pay special attention to any experiences that you may have while someone is passing or after they have passed. These can include unusual scents, sounds, visions, and coincidences. Also pay attention to dreams in which you are visiting with the person. My own clairvoyant experiences tell me that, as in life, after life people cannot help but be themselves. Watch for cues that are consistent with an individual's character and personality. Does the person show you familiar objects, sounds, or scents?
5. Consider reading books on the end of life, especially those that combine medical and spiritual perspectives, such as Peter and Elizabeth Fenwick's work.
6. The end of life represents an extraordinary opportunity to reflect on the ways in which the heavenly world *is* part of human existence, and how human existence *is* part of the heavenly world. Meditate on the correspondences that you perceive between these realms.
7. Never forget that love is the strongest force in the universe. Express your love and gratitude for everyone in your life, including those who are present, and those who are not.

## 37

# Seeing the End of Life as Part of the Total Creation: The Archangel Azrael

Azrael is the Archangel of Life, Death, and Creation. He can comfort us and help us to think and feel differently about the end of life, so that we see death not only as an integral part of life itself, but as part of a larger pattern of divine creation.

In both my professional work and in my personal life, I have often observed that people are profoundly uncomfortable with end of life issues. Frequently when colleagues or acquaintances hear about my work in palliative care, in their minds they start hoping, and even praying, that I will not discuss my experiences. When this occurs, I often hear their thoughts telepathically, and I can feel their responses viscerally as a twinge and a shudder in the midsection. Again and again I have seen that, in contemporary American culture, death remains the capital fear of many—if not most—people. While there can be great pain and suffering at the end of life, in all the years that I have been doing this work I have been amazed by the exquisite beauty and the boundless love that so often arise at this time. As I have been reflecting on my experiences, I have asked the Angels that some of the great power and delicacy of this pristine love be incorporated into this text so that an unexpected perspective on a difficult subject can be brought to light.

One evening, as I was relaxing quietly, I closed my eyes and prayed. I asked the heaven world that my words be allowed to help quell people's fears, so that they may know a little bit about the life that extends well beyond this lifetime. As I made this request, a vivid image came to mind. One of the Archangels I work with closely is Azrael. He tells me that he does not create souls, but that he creates creation itself, in this life and in the afterlife. Archangel Azrael is a Higher Being who can be extremely tall or extremely small, either masculine or feminine, serious or playful. He is more beautiful than I can describe, and he has a gentle but pointed sense of humor. He is so kind and graceful. When we communicated, he took on something like a human persona for my benefit. He tossed his head from one side to the other and looked me in the eye and said, *"Well now, my Dear..."* Then he took a wand, swirled it into a mist of colored light, and with the wand he made a figure eight, or infinity symbol, at the crown of my head. He told me that he was giving me a tiara of deep pink roses as a gift. Then he said that, when I first started doing the hospital work, during the first few weeks I was so nervous that I would do something wrong that "We on the other side were all amazed that your head didn't explode." And then we both laughed together.

When I asked him for an image for *The Angels In Between*, Azrael showed me a picture of myself standing in my living room with my arms stretched high above my head. My hands were reaching up to tug on the hem of his robe, which trails the Earth as it falls from the skies. As I said, Azrael can be very tall, and his presence extends into infinity. He himself is an infinity sign, and not only his power, but his beauty and gentleness, are unbelievable. He showed me that, when writing about end of life issues, through the energy of my words I was metaphorically tugging on the hem of his robe, the part of his garment that grazes the Earth. He said that I was a gentle scribe and servant, and he showed me that, when writing about these subjects, I was pulling back the edge of the hem of his garment, which was like pulling back a corner of the veil that separates *and* connects the earthly world and the heavenly one. Such encounters make me wonder how much love it is possible for the human heart to bear, and how much love can flow between realms. Azrael told me that this love "is the heart of the hereafter, which is the heart of the heart." This is the vision that I received through the veil between worlds, the veil that is the hem of Archangel Azrael's translucent garment, the membrane through which all life passes as the world is endlessly created and infinitely recreated.

### *Calling on the Archangel Azrael at the End of Life*

1. Know that Azrael is not only the Archangel of death, but of birth and creation. Practice seeing these transitions as different elements of life itself. Also know that Azrael is a source of infinite comfort, love, wisdom, gentleness, kindness, and goodness.
2. During periods of grief, call upon the Archangel Azrael to comfort you and wrap you in his soothing, cream-colored cloak. You can simply request this in your mind, or say the following prayer:

*Dear Azrael,*
*Please come to my side and bring me comfort.*
*Please send love into my heart so that I can accept this change*
*And see it as part of life's total creation.*
*Please surround my loved one with caring and comfort,*
*And please give me strength so that I can help both myself and others,*
*Especially those who need extra support at this time.*
*Thank you so much for your care and comfort,*
*And for the infinite gift of your presence.*
*Amen*

3. Open your heart as fully as possible to yourself, including being open not only to the pain and loss you may be experiencing, but to the beauty of the person's life and all the love you feel for them.
4. Consider repeating Azrael's words as a mantra to help you through transitional grieving. In your own mind, repeat the phrase:

*Love is the heart of the hereafter.*
*Love is the heart of the heart.*
*Amen.*

# 38

# Seeing Angels at the End of Life

While our culture often has great difficulty with this subject, the end of life can be a time when sacred and magical things occur. The stories contained in this section can help you to recognize and accept the extraordinary events that can arise in an end of life context, a time when Angels draw very close to the human beings they so lovingly attend.

In addition to my academic life at the university, since March of 2009 I have worked as an Artist In Residence on both the Acute Palliative Care Inpatient Unit and on the Palliative Care Outpatient Clinic at the M. D. Anderson Cancer Center. In this capacity, I work closely with people at the end of life and with their caregivers. My work is facilitated by the nonprofit organization COLLAGE: The Art for Cancer Network, which was conceived and founded by the oncologist Dr. Jennifer Wheler. At the hospital I assist people in constructing meaningful narratives to express their insights and experiences. Thus I primarily serve as a translator, yet much of what I translate is ineffable. I furnish a context, and contribute critical skills, so that people facing extraordinarily difficult life situations have an opportunity for personal and symbolic expression, which then becomes clothed in literary and poetic forms.

As an Artist In Residence, I constantly confront the challenge of creating human connections across a formidable gulf of separation. Sometimes when I initially approach a patient I am told that the work "sounds interesting, but I have no artistic ability." This invites me to respond, "Well, let's just say for a moment that you *did* have artistic ability. What images would you want to write about?" Depending on the circumstances I might also ask, "Where are you from?", "What do you love to do?", or even more simply (yet never simply), "What do you love?" Sometimes I will ask a person directly, "If you had an image in your mind of something that holds special meaning for you—and it can be anything at all—what would that be?" Very often these questions will inspire a flash of illumination, and the person will share an image with me. They will describe a subject or a scene, while I gently encourage them to talk and make notes to help crystallize their thoughts. Once the artwork is complete, I read the person's words back to them, while making any additions or corrections that they indicate. The narrative is then inscribed into a handmade paper journal, which the person can keep and share with their family, either as a medium for further creative expression or as a legacy gift that performs a memorial function. The portable microenvironment of the text thus provides a durable yet tender memory of this transient moment in a person's life.

In the fragile setting of acute palliative care, many surprising and wonderful things can arise—connections, coincidences, visions, and revelations. People come from all over the world to receive treatment at this renowned hospital, and over the years I have seen many extraordinary states of body, mind, and spirit. While I have also seen great pain and suffering, I have personally witnessed phenomena that can only be characterized as supernatural events and expressions of divine love. Each one has been powerful. I am now writing a book about my experiences as an Artist In Residence in palliative care, a study entitled *Words Beyond Words: Finding Language at the End of Life*. While in that text I tell many stories of spiritual and angelic presences, they are the patients' narratives, not my own. In this little book of *The Angels In Between*, I can share some of the many experiences that I have had while working in this extraordinary environment. Again, everything I describe is something that actually happened.

### *Above and Below*

One afternoon I was working on the ward and I saw an

extremely beautiful sight. A young woman lay in bed at the very end of her life. Her mother sat at the foot of her bed, holding her daughter's feet and rubbing her legs, attending her with great love and devotion. With equal love and caring, I was allowed to see a Guardian Angel at the head of the woman's bed. This Angel was an extremely bright silver-white color, and at first it looked like an orb or semi-circle of light. Then my vision sharpened and I saw that the Guardian Angel had long, vertical striations of light within its body, which resembled feathers. When I looked again I saw that the Angel's wings were outstretched and they were covering the young woman's head and shoulders from above. The Angel appeared to be perched on the young woman's pillow almost like a second, etheric headboard that lovingly screened, supported, protected, and soothed her. Thus this young woman was being held in love above and below, in both this world and beyond. A few moments after I entered the room, the young woman fell asleep peacefully. The sight was very tender and beautiful, although the mother's pain pierced straight through the heart. That day the circumstances did not permit me to share the vision that I was seeing. I truly wish I had been able to do so, because I feel that this image would have provided so much comfort.

### *"It's Beautiful in the Yard": The Flowers of St. Therese*

Oftentimes when doing this creative work, I have the strong sense that something beautiful is happening right now. One day I sat with an extremely elderly lady who spoke at length about the roses in her garden and the sacred associations these flowers held for her. As she told me:

**It's Beautiful in the Yard**

*I loved to work in the yard*
*With plants and things.*

*I had tulips and daisies and roses.*
*The roses were my favorites.*
*It was beautiful in the yard.*

*I'm Catholic, but I do my own thing.*
*The saint that is important to me is St. Therese.*
*She is known for the flowers.*
*I think of her when I see*
*The roses in my yard.*

After we finished the artwork, the frail woman turned to thank me. As I took her cold hand in my own, I could see the love of her garden shining in her eyes. Yet I was given another gift that afternoon as I witnessed a powerful angelic appearance.

Throughout the visit I had been sitting on the left-hand side of the woman's bed, close to the door. As I picked up my bag and turned to leave I saw that, just to the side of the chair in which I had been sitting for the past forty-five minutes was a very large column of electric silver-white light flashing brilliantly near the head of the bed. The flash lasted for only a moment, but it was clearly present and very powerful. I could also see that this woman was being attended to by this very bright angelic presence, and that she was being lovingly surrounded with pink roses. Once again, I had the sense that something beautiful was happening now.

Shortly after I wrote this story, I woke up one morning to the scent of roses. Lying in bed with my eyes still closed, I smelled the delicate, lemony, sweet fragrance of heavenly roses, and I knew that St. Therese and Mary Queen of the Angels were with me. With great love and tenderness, I sent a bouquet of roses back up to the sky, in gratitude for all the flowers that are sent to us here on earth.

## *Like a Bolt of Lighting*

One of the most dramatic supernatural occurrences I have ever experienced happened one afternoon when I visited an elderly African American lady. She told me that she is a devout Baptist, and as we conversed, it was clear that her faith was incredibly powerful. The artwork we produced together is entitled *An Extremely Bright Light,* which is this woman's image of divine presence:

**An Extremely Bright Light**

*There is an image on my mind.*
*It is my faith in God,*
*My Lord and Savior Jesus Christ.*
*I've had so many trials and tribulations,*
*But my faith got me through it.*
*When I think of my faith,*
*I think of the sun and of extremely bright light.*
*I think of anything that myself, or others, would find peaceful.*
*As I grow, it grows.*

*Once they had pronounced me dead,*
*But I came out of it.*
*He illuminates so that I can be of help to others.*
*When you see the light in me,*
*You see God working through me.*

As I sat inscribing the story, I was facing the woman who was lying in the bed, while a large square window was directly at my back. As I wrote the narrative, two powerful bolts of extremely bright silver-white light came shooting up fast behind me like lightning flashes. It was as though lightning actually came in through the window in back of me. The bolts leaped over my right shoulder and traveled horizontally into the heart of the woman lying in the bed. If I hadn't already had so many angelic experiences, I would have been frightened, as these were intense bolts of pure electricity, and they moved in a flash. When I turned around to look out the window, the sky outside was a clear, pure blue, and there were no clouds or signs of lightning anywhere.

## *Recognizing Angelic Presences and Attending People at the End of Life*

### *Preparing for the End of Life*

1. Recognize that extraordinary events can and do happen at transitional moments. Know that Angels accompany us at the end of life, which is a powerful point of transition.
2. Recall times in your life when you felt that something wonderful was about to happen, just before the experience began to unfold.
3. Reflect on stories that other people have shared about their own end of life experiences. See how their stories compare with yours.

### *Attending People at the End of Life*

1. Open your heart and your eyes to the person who is passing away. Know that this person is *the most important person in the room,* and allow them to be the center of care and attention. Also understand the deep connections between the living and the dying; realize that we all inhabit a single world.
2. Ask the person at the end of life if they have an image in their mind of something that holds special meaning or significance for them—and that it can be anything at all.

Make notes as they speak and record what they say as a way to honor the person. Their words will serve as a legacy gift to share with others.

3. When you are sitting with someone at the end of life, look at the head of their bed and see if you can discern extremely bright lights or fields of subtle moving energy. Pay careful attention to flashes of bright lights or sparkles of colorful lights by the bedside or in the corners of the room, and to any scents that you smell where the actual object—such as a flower—is not physically present.
4. Pay close attention to, and act on, your intuitive guidance. For example, notice if you are drawn to sit or stand in a particular location, or if you feel guided to ask the person if they would like their hand held, etc. Always respect their wishes as fully as possible. If the person does wish you to take their hand, look closely to see if you can discern angelic white light surrounding your two clasped hands.
5. Express gratitude for the gift of the person's life and the ability to be present at this moment.

# 39

# Accepting Extraordinary Events at Life's End: The Waterfall and the Waterwheel

Sometimes when I'm working at the hospital, I am able to reach people who otherwise seem to be beyond reach. As a clairvoyant, I follow my intuition and act on the guidance I am given in order to bridge worlds. The Angels attending the person will often tell me exactly where to stand, when to sit, and what to do. I follow their guidance as closely as possible, and I have been privileged to witness some incredible things.

### *The Other Side of the Waterfall*

Once I worked with the wife of a man who was very near the end of his life. She was delighted to spend time with an artist while she sat at her husband's bedside. She told me that he is of Native American heritage. While for several days he had lain in a semi-nonresponsive state, I could sense his tremendous presence of spirit and his great love for his wife. As we visited for well over an hour, this woman was in tears as she recalled the story of their first meeting and their courtship. These cherished memories formed the bases of the artwork we produced together, the centerpiece of which was a striking metaphorical image of...

**The Other Side of the Waterfall**

*With my husband, it was always an adventure,*
*Because I never knew where he was going to take me next.*
*Once we were up high in the mountains*
*And we were sitting together on the other side of a waterfall.*
*As we sat there looking out at the falling water*
*I knew that this was what I always wanted.*

Throughout our visit, the man remained unconscious. Yet when I asked the woman, "Can I read you the story that I just heard you tell?", her husband stirred in his bed. He briefly woke up, and he even sat up and swung his legs over the side of the bed. He became conscious and started smiling at her, and while he did not speak, he gestured and indicated that he very much wanted to hear the story. He and his wife sat together on the bed and looked at one another with great love while they received the artwork together. After I had finished reading, the man had to lie down again, and a few minutes later, he was nearly nonresponsive. It was as though this man had traveled back through the other side of the waterfall—that he briefly came through the curtain that separates realms of life and states of consciousness—in order to be present with his wife once again and sit with her, for just a few moments, on the other side of the waterfall.

Not only does this story present an intimate image of love, but it is an intriguing metaphor for end of life experience itself. While viewing the scene from "the other side of the waterfall," it is possible to see life from the opposite perspective than is customary, the reverse view of the world that normally appears before our eyes.

### *The Waterwheel*

While this man rested peacefully in his bed, there are other instances when the person is deeply frightened and in pain. On another occasion a nurse urged me to go into the room of an elderly lady who was very near death, who suffered from advanced dementia, and who had entered into a state of hypoactive delirium. Despite the medications she was receiving, this woman was still in a great deal of pain and she was fading away. While she was not capable of coherent conversation, when she looked up and saw me standing in the doorway, she looked directly into my eyes and said, "Please help me. Will you help me? Help me, help me." The nurse told her my name and the woman said, "Marcia, will you help me?" I assured her that, of course I would help her. When the nurse asked her what she would like, the woman really couldn't answer. She could barely speak, and even small gestures were such an effort for her. This was one of the first occasions when I had to work almost entirely intuitively, and this woman and I had an incredible exchange primarily off the verbal level. I sat at her bedside, and I asked her if my sitting there would help her. She said yes. Once we had made contact, she said to me, "Just talk. Just tell me things." So I told her a true story about what helps me. I told her that, when I went out for a walk the previous afternoon, I saw a female woodpecker. I described how this large bird had such a gentle face and such distinctive black and white markings. I told the woman how I had seen the bird on a tree limb at a distance, and how I approached it very slowly and carefully, so that I could get as close to the bird as possible. That way I could approach this shy, gentle presence, just as I was doing with her right now. The woman liked this story, and I asked if these words helped her. She nodded and smiled, and then we worked without words.

Very gently, I took the woman's hand and I could feel that she was in terrible pain. I felt the pain throughout her body especially streaming through the tingling and trembling of her third and fourth fingers. Without words I told her that it was okay to release this pain, to give it to me and let it go completely. This woman cried while she released her pain. While the pain came through in irregular spasms, at one point there was a particularly severe wave and the woman called out, "Oh, someone's hurting." I could tell that, through her own pain, she was reconnecting with other people's pain that she had witnessed and absorbed in her lifetime. All the while I could feel that my own Angelic Guides were standing at my back with their hands on my shoulders. We were all deeply connected, and an enormous amount of energy passed through me. My cheeks were flushed and both of my hands were running hot. The woman too felt the heat, and she commented, "Oh, that's hot." We worked together for quite a while, until she stabilized, and things were in a much more peaceful place. I could feel everything, and I knew when our work together was done. At the end of the visit, the woman's pain had pulled back and she was infused with a sense of peace. I have asked the Angels to take as much of my light as possible to help reach those who cannot be reached otherwise. Again, the privilege of doing this work is truly beyond words.

A little while later I was discussing this encounter with Pat McKenna. Through her, the Angelic Guides gave their perspective on what had occurred. As they said, "When you touched, your hearts were one. You took the fear and sloughed it through you and off of you. The exhibit of the woman's fear came up and showed itself as a black-gray form that came to you and shattered completely into tiny little pieces, into insignificant particles that disappeared in a poof, all three million of them. It's not around you and it's not around her, and this is the point: *she did not take it with her*. It will never happen that you cannot transform. You are the waterwheel that would move the giant stone to grind the corn or wheat. You will always have all of the energy, and all of the beauteous beings that you need, to help people who are alone and need to have clarity. You transmutate through your own system, like a luminescent bubble that lifts from your soul, like a bubble that comes off of a wand and lifts everything into the light pale colors of gold and silver. The bubble leaves you and lifts whatever the person cannot take along. It lifts, and then it is gone."

### *Accepting Extraordinary Events at Life's End*

1. Read the stories in this section carefully and reflect on them deeply. While they represent my experiences as a seasoned clairvoyant medium who regularly works with

people at the end of life, just by reading the words and opening your eyes and your heart to the images, you will understand more of what can happen at the end of life, including the extraordinary dimensions of death's mysteries and its sacred beauty. Perhaps beyond all else, try to remain open to the open, because you can never, ever tell what will happen at the end of life.

2. As you attend a person at the end of life, practice seeing their aura. Then, look closely to see how, or if, the light of their spirit still corresponds to their physical body. Are they emanating extremely large amounts of bright light and energy, and are their physical and light bodies beginning to detach from one another? If you are allowed to see the light of a person's soul coming forth, give thanks with all your heart. This is a life transforming experience, and you will never be the same again.

# 40

# Attending People at the End of Life and Helping Them to Leave with Grace: A Material Medium

When I work with people at the end of life, we'll talk, we'll often laugh, and sometimes we'll cry together. Typically I will sit with a person and we will visit together, while on other occasions we sit in total silence, holding hands, and a great deal of energy passes between us. I can feel the energy running like a live current through the channel of my body and goose-flesh will often rise on my arms. As the great British medium Ena Twigg used to say, "I just bring the body," and then I sit back in the chair while the Angelic Guides do the work.

In my own mind, one of the phrases I use to describe this healing work is that I serve not only as an Artist In Residence, but as a material medium for people at the end of life. Because I am a human being who is alive and attuned to the human, angelic, and elemental realms, I can often help bring many worlds together while grounding etheric energies physically in the material domain. I work with eight Angelic Master Guides, and they are all absolutely incredible. When I do this work, we all walk as one. Very often when I'm visiting with people, the Angelic Guides will impress into my mind what I need to say to someone, or what the person needs to hear. Then as I sit and talk, people will see me differently. Sometimes as they look at me, it's as though my physical appearance changes, and my facial features and even my clothing will shift before their eyes. Depending on the person's background and the circumstances in which they grew up, the person in the bed might see me wearing a Greek or French or Italian outfit from many decades ago. And while I am always speaking English, the person might hear what

I'm saying in Greek or in French or Italian. The Angelic Guides tell me that, when this occurs, the person is linking to their truth and to something that they may have lost from childhood. During such visits, I can feel the energies both within myself and within the other person flowing and transforming all around us. After such an experience, the person will typically be in a state of deep relaxation, and very often, they will be filled with peace and joy.

In addition to this creative communication work, the Angelic Guides often use me as a conductor, as a kind of human extension cord that strengthens and amplifies the connection between worlds so that, in these very delicate situations, the light can go wherever it needs to go in a very human and materially grounded way. While I hold people's hands, an energy current is conducted through my physical body, and this energetic flow strengthens the sense of spirit presence in both the physical body and the spirit of the person. Sometimes the energies are extremely light and delicate and they feel almost nonexistent; at other times, the energies are running hot and I will become very flushed while we work together. I can never predict in advance what will happen. Thus I stand in the middle of things, *in media res*. As an Artist In Residence I not only work with artistic media, but I am an artistic "medium," or form of creative material, for the Angelic Guides to work with. As both a spiritual and an artistic medium, I stand within and between many worlds simultaneously.

At the physical level, when I hold a person's hand and a tremendous amount of energy is moved through me, part of what is occurring is that my own wonderful Body Elemental is connecting physically and spiritually with the Body Elemental of the person suffering from the disease. This provides the person with an added measure of physical strength and support. Very often with terminal cancer patients, when I first take a person's hand, it feels as if they are trembling, sometimes slightly and sometimes violently. Almost always, at the end of life it seems like there are frayed connections and broken threads in the person's electrical circuitry, all of which destabilize the body even further. After holding the person's hand for a while, I can feel that these energetic threads are stronger and steadier, and only once after I have left a patient's room was the person still trembling. As a material medium, it is my privilege to help ground angelic presences in the material world, so that I can help to cleanse a situation, turn negative energies around, and lift the light up as high as possible. As always, the Angelic Guides do all the real heavy lifting.

Sometimes doing this work gives me an unearthly feeling. It's as though I am partially out of my body and floating up near the ceiling. The person's Guides and Angels use me as a vehicle, and a lot of molecules are moved through me by these angelic forces. When this happens, the heaviness surrounding the person gradually disappears, and the light of their soul comes through. I have found that, when women experience this, they often giggle with joy. And when men experience this, they are often taken aback and completely blown away. I can hear them thinking, *"Oh My God"*, because they may never have experienced such uplift before.

### *Light Streaming From My Hands*

I have also noticed that, as I sit quietly inscribing people's stories into the handmade paper journals, a very bright, silver-white light will often emanate from my hands and fingertips. When this occurs, it's as though my physical body is a conductor and transmitter of light. Much like the aura, the movement of the light corresponds exactly with the movements of my hands and it becomes infused into the ink, the paper, and the words themselves. Then I can actually see the light going into the journals. This does not always happen in the same way during each visit. On some days it may be that I am allowed to carry especially strong amounts of white light because that is what is needed at the time.

### *A Halo of Hands*

Recently, I saw something that I have never witnessed before. With my physical eyes, I was shown that, as I held a woman's hands firmly in my own two hands, an Angel gently placed its hand atop of ours. The Angel's hand was extended flat, with its palm down, over our clasped fingers. The Angel's hand was composed of extremely delicate bright white light. It was unbelievably beautiful, and its touch was so soft. As the Angel's hand rested atop our fingers, strengthening and blessing the connection, it looked as though our own interwoven human hands were haloed in radiant white light.

# 41

# Seeing a Human Soul: The Light Separating from the Body

Every human being has a soul, and sometimes we are privileged to be allowed to see it. This vision can change our lives, forever.

When people are in their final days or hours, I am sometimes allowed to see the light of the person's soul separating from their physical body. This occurrence is so beautiful that it is nearly impossible to find words to describe this indescribable event, even though my job is to find the words. One powerful example that I will never forget came the day I visited with an exceptionally elderly man. His body was so thin and frail, and his face was so swollen with tumors that he could barely speak. Yet he wanted me by his side. He wanted to visit for a while and tell me about his life. While this man was very close to death, he was not at all in a state of crisis. Rather, he emanated a supreme sense of peace and serenity. I sat quietly by his side for a long time, just giving gentle support, watching closely and listening to him. After a while, I asked if I could hold his hand. I held his right hand in my left, and his grip was surprisingly strong, given how weak and frail he was.

After about an hour of sitting quietly together, I saw an incredibly powerful glowing aura of golden, bright silver-white, and pale blue light surrounding this man's body. The light appeared to be rising up from his heart. It resembled the auras that I describe in this book, but it was many times brighter in magnitude and arrestingly beautiful. It was constantly shifting, like a fluid electromagnetic field. It was the largest, brightest human aura I've ever seen. The Angelic Guides informed me that, because it was this man's wish, I was being allowed to see the light of his soul. When the sunlight shone against his pillow, I could see the light even more clearly.

The contrasts between realities were so extreme and striking. This elderly man's body was so fragile, stricken, and ill, and yet the light of his soul was so intense, pristine, and powerful. The soul appeared as pure light, pure energy, pure presence, and pure beauty. This man's soul seemed to be separating from his body in real time before my eyes. In addition to his soul, I could also see the light of his Guardian Angel and other attending Angels of Transition as beaming haloes of light all around him. It was so beautiful because I knew that, as I sat in that hospital room with that man, I also sat at a point where the earthly and the heavenly worlds were actively converging, *and I knew that the link between worlds was not only exceptionally beautiful but that it was powerfully alive.* Like that day so long ago when I first saw auras while standing in line at the Post Office, all I could do was sit in wonder while I silently expressed love and gratitude.

After a while, I asked this man if he would like to rest. He said no and asked me to stay, "because I'll have plenty of time to rest soon." At the end of our visit, when I turned to say goodbye, he said to me, "Maybe I'll spot you some time." Thus with very few words and more than a tinge of humor, this man expressed his recognition of his own end of life situation and of the continuation of life in the afterlife. As I turned to walk out the door, I blew this man a kiss. He showed me that he caught it and he sent one back, which I caught and which I have never let go.

# VI

# How to Live like a Light Carrier

# 42

# Joining the Community of Light Carriers: The Hollow Straw

A community of Light Carriers is living and working on the planet right now. You can actively cultivate this connection by listening receptively to your Angelic Guides, by practicing the art of allowance, and by remaining open to the open, open to the mystical possibilities of being in many places at once. Through such openings you can send powerful prayers to others, while acting as a Light Carrier.

Sometimes practicing the art of allowance can be very difficult. Sometimes admitting the full range of what we know, see, and feel—and by this, I mean admitting this to ourselves, let alone to others—can be a very difficult thing. In one way, it would be so much easier if we could all just stick to a comfortable, predetermined storyline. Yet if we were to do this, we would never truly be the authors of our own stories. Instead, we would be living out someone else's drama, and I know that I, for one, am certainly not here for that purpose.

It is always necessary to exercise discernment regarding what to say to whom and when, and when to remain silent, in order to make wise judgments regarding how much to share with others. There are times when groups of people with diverse opinions and perspectives must work together, and you cannot automatically trust how people will respond, nor can you necessarily count on others to be supportive. Instead, you should trust the wisdom of your own internal guidance and honor your own deepest sense of the truth of what you know.

This sense of constantly having to hold yourself back—and remain in the clairvoyant closet—can be extremely frustrating. This condition can easily lead to a situation where you feel alone and lonely. The Angelic Guides reassure us that none of us are ever alone, that we are always accompanied and deeply loved. They want you to know that you have Angels and Guides working with you right now, at this very moment. Once you recognize this consciously, all you have to do is ask for assistance and pray for guidance. Then pause, listen, and be receptive to what comes to you in life. The Angels also emphasize that, not only are they always with you, but just as importantly, you are always connected to the wisdom of your own soul, which is ever-present and full of light. Again, they ask you to consider the question: How would you live your life differently if you knew that angelic assistance was always available? How would you live your life differently if you felt accompanied and absolutely loved?

The Angels tell me that there are many, many Light Carriers who are alive and working right now on this planet, human beings who form a community of living light. Knowing of my great love of flowers, the Angelic Guides show me a vision of the radiant love that emanates from the Light Bearers who are here on missions of love, devotion, passion, and compassion. The love and dedication of those who are here right now are like bouquets of light that blossom everywhere on the planet, in every sweet color, form, and fragrance imaginable.

The Guides tell me that this radiance is interconnected, and this light forms a kind of living community for those who are here on mission, yet who feel alone. The Angelic Guides tell me emphatically, yet with a smile, that the light is alive, and that we are all expressions of living light.

How do we access these interconnections? Let me answer this question with another question: Do you remember when you were a child and, as a special treat, you were taken out for an ice cream sundae or a milkshake? I certainly can. When I was young, my parents liked to visit a particular ice cream parlor in a local shopping mall. I remember one evening when, after my parents had finished their shopping, they stopped by this shop and we all ordered milkshakes. Mine was strawberry, and I can still see with absolute clarity the gleaming silver milkshake cup, the high, frosted parfait glass with the scalloped glass edges, and the soft pink pastel swirls of the strawberry milkshake. The milkshake came with a white straw, and I can remember blissfully sipping the pink ice cream up through the straw and feeling all the sweet flavors and cold textures melt in my mouth and slide down my throat.

The Angels ask us to pause and consider the straw in this story, that important transitional element between two points that serves as the open passageway that makes this experience possible. The Angels tell me that the straw is a channel, and that here on this planet there are many Light Workers who are also hollow straws through which energy and information can pass freely. Like the straw, Light Workers can help to channel energies, to connect various dimensions of being, and to serve as a living corridor within and between worlds. The Angels emphasize that the straw is both solid and hollow, and this is extremely important because both attributes are necessary to fulfill its function. Another way to think about this is that, by being both solid and hollow, the straw at once contains a presence and an absence. By incorporating multiple states simultaneously, the straw is able to serve as a useful instrument and as an open channel that bridges the distance between two points, while connecting what is above with what is below—just as Light Workers do.

### *Receiving Angelic Guidance and Intuitive Information*

1. Listen closely to your Angelic Guides and to your own intuitive guidance. When you have a question or you face a situation where you need guidance, enter into a meditative state. Then breathe deeply, ask for assistance,

and pray for guidance. Pause, wait, and listen to the information that comes forth. Practice listening to the "still, small voice within." Pay attention to how this information makes you feel. Can you discern that this guidance is for the highest good of all involved? Give thanks for the insight you receive.

2. Sip a drink slowly through a hollow straw and notice how the straw connects one point with another, bridging two worlds. Both in your meditation and in your life, practice being the hollow straw that bridges two locations, a channel through which energy can flow freely.
3. Know that, as you actively live in the light to help and serve others, you are not alone. A community of Light Carriers is living on this planet right now and working for the highest good of all. Practicing the exercises in this book will help cultivate and strengthen your abilities as a Light Worker.
4. Particularly when facing difficult choices, remain true to yourself and be in your integrity. Call upon your own Angelic Guides and the Archangel Michael for additional courage when you face challenging situations.
5. Do you live and work in a supportive community that is open to the unseen worlds, or do you repeatedly find that you need to be cautious and discreet in your interactions with others? Do not automatically expect others to be supportive of your perspective, particularly if your spiritual and personal beliefs are different from their own. Exercise care and discernment regarding what you choose to share. Know when to speak, and when to remain silent.
6. If you are feeling alone and lonely, know that your Angels are with you at all times, every step of the way. Allow their presences to enter your life as fully as

possible, and thank them for always being there, always sending you love. Send your love back to them, and feel this golden light flow through the hollow straw of your being.

## 43

# Contributing to the Bank of Light

We are all channels of divine light. The Angelic Guides ask us to consider the various ways in which we all bring worlds together in our lives, and how we serve as a channel through which goodness flows freely. This too represents another beautiful spiritual paradox, that of self-affirmation through self-overcoming. Let me give you another example of how to put this into practice.

I watch very little television. However, one program that I do try to watch regularly is the PBS NewsHour. This show features so many important stories and offers thoughtful debates on extremely complex issues. The program provides coverage of both national and global news, some of which is extremely difficult to watch. In so many places our planet is experiencing natural and humanitarian disasters. It is incredibly hard to witness such large-scale human and environmental suffering. Moreover, it is extremely frustrating to feel like a helpless bystander, with the empty sense that there is nothing useful that we can do. In fact, there *is* something that we can do, and this act can be very powerful.

One evening, after witnessing yet another story of heart-breaking devastation, I found myself asking the Angels if there weren't some small way that I could be of service. Shortly thereafter, inspiration came through a compelling angelic suggestion. The Angels showed me a vision of a bank of light. We are all familiar with the World Bank and with other investment banks that provide global financial assistance, and we all know of the agencies and organizations that supply needed humanitarian relief. Yet the Angels showed me that there is also another kind of bank that is filled, not with the hard material currencies of silver and gold, but with the soft, etheric splendor of the light of the soul, the golden light of love, the silver light of devotion, and the white light of grace. This bank resembles a repository that holds an endless pool of light, a glowing reservoir of compassion and love.

To contribute to this heavenly bank of light, the Angels gave me the following prayer. They tell me how pleased they are that this prayer is being shared. If you feel guided to contribute, before falling asleep at night you can say the following words:

*Dear Angels,*

*In the dreamtime,*
*Please take the light of my soul*
*And allow it to be used*
*For the highest good of all.*

*Please allow my soul to work with the Angels*
*So that I may be of the greatest assistance*
*Wherever help is needed.*
*Please allow me to travel freely,*
*So that I may love and serve others.*
*I release unto You the need to determine*
*Where and how I may serve.*
*Please add my light to the larger bank of light,*
*So that as I lay asleep in the darkness,*
*The light of grace and blessings may fall*
*To light the darkness*
*Of others here on Earth.*
*Thank you so much for hearing my prayer.*

*Amen*

## *Praying for Others*

1. Consciously practice becoming the hollow straw, a channel for the flow of divine light and goodness. Consider how you bring multiple worlds together in your life.
2. Know that, as a Light Bearer, you are able to send powerful prayers to others. The next time you hear about a natural or humanitarian disaster—this can be any situation where people are in pain and need help—consider saying this prayer before you fall asleep at night:

*Dear Angels,*

*In the dreamtime,*
*Please take the light of my soul*
*And allow it to be used*
*For the highest good of all.*

*Please allow my soul to work with the Angels*
*So that I may be of the greatest assistance*
*Wherever help is needed.*
*Please allow me to travel freely,*
*So that I may love and serve others.*
*I release unto You the need to determine*
*Where and how I may serve.*
*Please add my light to the larger bank of light,*
*So that as I lay asleep in the darkness,*
*The light of grace and blessings may fall*
*To light the darkness*
*Of others here on Earth.*
*Thank you so much for hearing my prayer.*

*Amen*

When you wake up the next morning, pay careful attention to how you feel. Do you feel any different than usual, or do you recall any particular images? The changes may be subtle, so look closely.

3. Consciously recognize that, as you perform these exercises, you are contributing to the heavenly bank of light, and you are living as a Light Carrier. Give thanks for the gift of being allowed to serve in this way.

# 44

# "When You Look in the Mirror, You're Looking at Me": How to Recognize the Angel Within

As you recognize yourself as a Light Carrier, you grow closer to your Angelic Guides. You also start taking responsibility for your life in a new way as you actively acknowledge that you, too, are here to make a difference.

Many years ago, when I first started exploring metaphysical subjects, I asked how I could grow closer to my own Angelic Guides. The answer I received absolutely shocked me. I was told, "We are already so close. When you look in the mirror, you're looking at me."

At the time I was not yet ready to accept this wisdom, so I told myself various stories of disavowal. They went something like this: "Hmmm, that just can't possibly be right. Isn't that interesting, how they can make mistakes in the heaven world just like they do here on earth." Another tale of denial went like this: "Okay, obviously this Angel is just being really nice to me. That's probably its official job, anyway. This Angel must be like someone's grandmother who pays extravagant compliments even when they're not true." There were other stories as well, but those are the ones I remember the best. While all of those years ago I was not yet ready to fully accept, let alone embrace, the possibility of angelic and human communion, the important point is that the Angels had planted the idea in my mind, and the image gave me a sense of absolute joy, elation and wonder. This story is typical of how I repeatedly questioned myself and how, over the years, I opened my mind and my heart again and again. Each experience has made me a better person, and I am so grateful for everything that I have been shown.

How much of this story is familiar to you? If you have a loving heart, then it is very likely that you are here to make a difference. Passionate love is about helping others, and compassionate love is about giving to others. Both types of love help to create a sense of balance and equity on this planet, and the Angels tell me that we all walk in this light.

Once when I was walking through the lovely Japanese Garden in Houston's Hermann Park, I came to a small wooden footbridge that was suspended delicately over a pool of shimmering water. As I paused in the middle of the bridge, I noticed that some turtles were partially submerged in the water, and partially sunning themselves on the rocks. Turtles can walk on the land as gracefully as they swim in the water. They have one foot in one world, and one foot in another, and they live in multiple worlds at once.

The Angels tell me that Light Carriers are vehicles that are enamored with divine love and being of assistance to other beings. How sweet it is that memories come back of being both here and there, of having one leg in heaven and one on earth. Yet just as we have one leg in one world, and one leg in another, we have one heart that does the work and says to other people, "You are not small. You are as beautiful as the sun in the morning and the moon at night." Showing people the beauty of their own light gives so much hope. Love is ever-abounding and boundless. It is an easy give-away, because everyone wants it.

Love is all ways and always. Both versions of this phrasing are so important: *Love is All Ways and Always.* Holding that thought is thinking like an Angel.

### *Recognizing the Angel Within*

1. Recognize your connection with the Angels, who are always so close, closer than you think. Consciously affirm that, like the Angels, you too are here to make a difference.

2. In meditation, ask your Angelic Guides how you can grow closer to them. Pay careful attention to the guidance you receive, and to your immediate and long-term responses. Are you shy when approaching your Angels, or are you happy and self-confident? Do their words inspire awe, elation, and wonder? How many of their suggestions concern ways in which you can clean up your life? Do they offer guidance on how you can help and give to others? Do they show you ways that you can discreetly show other people their own beauty? How do you respond to these angelic ideas? Do you resist these suggestions? Do you need a little time to process angelic wisdom before acting on it? Be patient with yourself. An angelic perspective may be quite unlike a human one. Give yourself ample time to become familiar, not only with angelic presences, but with angelic ways of thinking. As you do, you will come to see the world in a different light—and you will recognize yourself in a different light, as well.
3. As you practice these modes of living and thinking, do you find that you are simultaneously walking in multiple worlds at once? How does mysticism manifest in your life?
4. As always, express gratitude for the gift of your life and the growth of your soul, which unfolds through your efforts of dedication and conscious recognition.

# 45

# Unfurling Our Wings: The Closing Ceremony

Although this book is written in the first person, this story is not just about me. Above all, it is about helping the work to go forward. This book is about helping you to understand that you have Angels who are always available to you and who always love you, and that goodness is here, goodness is now, and goodness is you. You are never alone. You are always accompanied by the light of divine love. Please accept your worthiness to be doing this work. Part of this entails recognizing and accepting the perfection of unconditional love, which lives in you and in me and in all beings. While we are all human and we all make errors from time to time, our souls can only be perfect in the eyes of our Angels.

After I finished writing this book, the Angelic Guides instructed me to undertake a six hour ceremony. This is heavy duty ritual work! Part of this experience entailed performing some ceremonial functions with lighted candles, while part of this involved entering into extended states of prayer and meditation, and yet another part consisted of working with creative imagery to construct a power symbol for this book. I was told that the six hours were necessary for the solid construction of a sacred space. Writing this book is like building a house made of light.

As I sat in meditation, the words and imagery appeared. First, I was told that books have the potential to change people's lives. I was shown that people grow stronger, and the light grows brighter, as we all learn from our experiences. This is a gift to everyone.

Then in my mind's eye, it appeared as though I was standing

outside of myself looking down on the scene in my room. I saw myself sitting at my maple desk with a typescript copy of *The Angels In Between* directly before me, and my arms encircled the text as I prayed and meditated. Yet I saw that not only did I sit at the desk, but that a set of Angel wings was wrapped around the text, forming a circle that extended beyond my hands and enclosed the book at the center of the prayer. Then I saw that, while the book and my hands were at the center, many other Angel wings were also wrapped around the text. The Angels' wings looked like flickering flames of light. It was as though there were concentric rings of radiant Angel wings, all mutually enclosing one another and fanning outwards to form a consolidated circle of light. All of the Angel wings were luminous, protective, mutually embracing forms that encircled one another in an enormous ring of light. As the Angels prayed, more Angels joined in, with layer after layer of wings encircling wings.

Then I saw that the ring of light that surrounded the book was expanding outwards to create a vortex of energy that formed an open channel or pathway that cut through the heavy, dense atmosphere of the earth. It's almost as if books such as *The Angels In Between* are holding open a patch of bright blue sky, just as the book is a window opening onto other worlds. And just as the concentric rings of angelic presences created an opening of light, this luminous, protective opening is a channel of love. You, too, are within this opening, within this vortex of light. I was told that reading books such as this, and taking their lessons to heart, creates a holy opening in the thick atmosphere of this planet. As you sit holding this book in your hands, imagine the layers of etheric Angel wings spread out in front of you as concentric rings of light, with you sitting at the center. This is a channel for the goodness of divine love, and your life is an opening through which this love can flow.

Together we are creating an opening through which this influx of light becomes an everyday occurrence in the world. As the Angels tell me, when we open our minds, we open our hearts and our eyes, and then we know that it is possible to change the future through the power of love.

### *Unfurling Your Wings*

1. Consider how the stories in this book do, or do not, resonate with you. Allow both responses to be valid and learn from the comparisons.
2. Repeat the following affirmation, "I am always loved and accompanied by Angels. Goodness is here, goodness is now, goodness is me and goodness is you, now and always."
3. Consider the books and ideas that have changed your life. What are they, and do you recognize a pattern among them? What did you learn from these stories, and how do you apply this knowledge in your life?
4. When you perform an act of love or generosity, what are the consequences? Does the energy ripple outward like a stone thrown into a pond? How does this opening create additional openings, both for yourself and for others?
5. As you sit reading this book, imagine that you are surrounded by ranks of Angels with outstretched wings who read the book with you and who hold open a channel of love and light. Can you sense these angelic presences? How does this vision make you feel?
6. Recognize, and give thanks, for the eternal power of love. Lift up your heart and your eyes.

# References

Atwood, Mary Dean. *Spirit Healing: Native American Magic & Medicine.* New York: Sterling Publishing, 1991.

*Bell, Book, and Candle.* Directed by Richard Quine. New York: Columbia Pictures, 1958.

*The Bishop's Wife.* Directed by Henry Koster. New York: RKO Pictures, 1947.

Brennan, Marcia. *The Day Your Heart Broke In Your Eyes: The Book of Recognition.* Nevada City, CA: Blue Dolphin Publishing, 2011.

Brennan, Marcia. *Words Beyond Words: Finding Language at the End of Life.* Bristol, UK: Intellect Books, forthcoming.

Byrne, Lorna. *Stairways to Heaven.* London: Hodder & Stoughton, 2010.

Fenwick, Peter and Elizabeth Fenwick. *The Art of Dying: A Journey to Elsewhere.* London: Continuum, 2008.

Rembrandt van Rijn, *Zacharias and the Angel,* c. 1635. Brown ink on paper. Fogg Art Museum, Harvard University Art Museums, Cambridge, MA.

Twigg, Ena and Ruth Hagy Brod. *Ena Twigg: Medium.* New York: Hawthorn Books, 1972.

AXIS MUNDI
BOOKS

Axis Mundi Books provide the most revealing and coherent explorations and investigations of the world of hidden or forbidden knowledge. Take a fascinating journey into the realm of Esoteric Mysteries, Magic, Mysticism, Angels, Cosmology, Alchemy, Gnosticism, Theosophy, Kabbalah, Secret Societies and Religions, Symbolism, Quantum Theory, Apocalyptic Mythology, Holy Grail and Alternative Views of Mainstream Religion.